SOLO!

The Best Monologues of the 80s (Men)

THE ACTOR AND THE TEXT
Cicely Berry

SHAKESCENES: SHAKESPEARE FOR TWO
John Russell Brown

SHAKESPEARE'S PLAYS IN PERFORMANCE
John Russell Brown

ACTING IN FILM
(book & videocassette)
Michael Caine

A PERFORMER PREPARES
David Craig

ON SINGING ONSTAGE
David Craig

STANISLAVSKY TECHNIQUE: RUSSIA
Mel Gordon

THE END OF ACTING: A RADICAL VIEW
Richard Hornby

DIRECTING THE ACTION
Charles Marowitz

RECYCLING SHAKESPEARE
Charles Marowitz

MICHAEL CHEKHOV:
ON THEATRE AND THE ART OF ACTING
(audiotapes)

STANISLAVSKI REVEALED
Sonia Moore

THE MONOLOGUE WORKSHOP
Jack Poggi

THE CRAFTSMEN OF DIONYSUS
Jerome Rockwood

SPEAK WITH DISTINCTION
Edith Skinner

CREATING A CHARACTER
Moni Yakim

The Best Monologues of the 80s (Men)

Edited by
Michael Earley and Philippa Keil

APPLAUSE
THEATRE BOOK PUBLISHERS

SOLO! The Best Monologues of the 80's (Men)
Copyright © 1987 by Applause Theatre Book Publishers
Acting Solo and *Your Sixty Seconds of Fame* copyright © 1987
by Michael Earley

The acknowledgements pages constitute an extension of this
copyright page.

Library of Congress Cataloging-in-Publication Data

Solo! : the best monologues of the 80's (men).

   (The Applause Acting Series)
   Summary: presents a collection of powerful monologues for
actors, written by the decade's most influential and popular
dramatists from the United States and Great Britain.
   1. Monologues. 2. Acting. 3. Actors. 4. American drama—20th
century. 5. English Drama—20th century. [1. Monologues. 2.
Acting. 3. American drama—20th century. 4. English drama—
20th century.] I. Earley, Michael. II. Keil, Philippa. III. Series.
PN2080.S65 1987 812'.045'08 87-17476
ISBN 0-936839-65-1 (pbk.)

British Library Cataloging-in-Publication Data

A catalogue record for this book is available from the British
Library

APPLAUSE BOOKS

211 West 71st Street, New York, NY 10023
Phone: 212-595-4735, Fax: 212-721-2856

406 Vale Road, Tonbridge KENT TN9 1XR
Phone: 0732 357755, Fax: 0732 770219

ACKNOWLEDGEMENTS

Grateful acknowledgement is made for permission to reprint excerpts from copyrighted material:

ALBUM by David Rimmer. Copyright © as an unpublished dramatic composition by David Rimmer, 1980. Copyright © David Rimmer 1981. Reprinted by permission of the author.

AMADEUS by Peter Shaffer. Copyright © Peter Shaffer, 1980 and 1981. Reprinted by permission of the author's agent, Robert Lantz, The Lantz Office, 888 Seventh Avenue, New York, NY 10106.

THE AMERICAN CLOCK by Arthur Miller. Copyright © Arthur Miller, 1982. Reprinted by permission of International Creative Management, 40 West 57th Street, New York, NY 10019.

ASINAMALI! by Mbongeni Ngema. Copyright © Mbongeni Ngema, 1986. Reprinted by permission of George Braziller, Inc., 60 Madison Avenue, New York, NY 10010.

AS IS by William M. Hoffman. Copyright © William M. Hoffman, 1985. Reprinted by permission of Random House Inc., 201 East 50th Street, New York, NY 10022.

AZTEC by John O'Keefe. Copyright © John O'Keefe, 1986. Reprinted by permission of the author.

BATTERY by Daniel Therriault. Copyright © Daniel Therriault, 1983. Reprinted by permission of the author.

BODIES by James Saunders. Copyright © James Saunders, 1979. Reprinted by permission of the author. All rights whatsoever in this play are strictly reserved and application for performance etc. should be made before rehearsal to Margaret Ramsay Ltd., 14a Goodwin's Court, St. Martin's Lane, London WC2N 4LL, England.

THE BODY by Nick Darke. Copyright © Nick Darke, 1983. Reprinted by permission of Methuen London Ltd., 11 New Fetter Lane, London EC4P 4EE, England.

BOPHA! by Percy Mtwa. Copyright © Percy Mtwa, 1986. Reprinted by permission of George Braziller, Inc., 60 Madison Avenue, New York, NY 10010.

BORDERLINE by Hanif Kureishi. Copyright © Hanif Kureishi, 1981. Reprinted by permission of Methuen London Ltd., 11 New Fetter Lane, London EC4P 4EE, England.

BRIGHTON BEACH MEMOIRS by Neil Simon. Copyright © Neil Simon 1984. Reprinted by permission of the author and Random House, Inc., 201 East 50th Street, New York, NY 10022.

CONTENTS

INTRODUCTION: ACTING SOLO
by Michael Earley   1

YOUR SIXTY SECONDS OF FAME
by Michael Earley   6

MONOLOGUES (Guide to Genre/Age Range)

ALBUM
David Rimmer (comic/16)   23

AMADEUS
Peter Shaffer (serious/30s-40s)   24

THE AMERICAN CLOCK
Arthur Miller (serious/60s-70s)   26

ASINAMALI!
Mbongeni Ngema (seriocomic/20s/Black)   27

AS IS
William M. Hoffman (serious/30s)   29

AZTEC
John O'Keefe (seriocomic/20s-40s)   30

BATTERY
Daniel Therriault (comic/20s-30s)   32

BODIES
James Saunders (serious/30s-40s)   34

THE BODY
Nick Darke (seriocomic/18-20s)   37

BOPHA!
Percy Mtwa (serious/20s/Black)   38

BORDERLINE
Hanif Kureishi (serious/19-20s/Indian)   40

BRIGHTON BEACH MEMOIRS
Neil Simon (comic/16)   41

CHILDREN OF A LESSER GOD
Mark Medoff (serious/30s)   42

CLOUD NINE
Caryl Churchill (seriocomic/30s)   43

THE COLORED MUSEUM
George C. Wolfe (seriocomic/20s-30s/Black)   44

DANCING BEARS
Stuart Browne (serious/20s-30s)   46

DANNY AND THE DEEP BLUE SEA
John Patrick Shanley (serious/20s-30s)   48

THE DRESSER (2)
Ronald Harwood (seriocomic/serious/30s-40s)   50

THE ELEPHANT MAN
Bernard Pomerance (serious/30s)   53

END OF THE WORLD
Arthur Kopit (serious/40s)   54

FENCES (2)
August Wilson (serious/50s/Black)   56

FIVE OF US
Len Jenkin (comic/20s-30s)   58

FOB
David Henry Hwang (seriocomic/20s/Asian`   60

FOOL FOR LOVE (2)
Sam Shepard (seriocomic/50s-70s/serious/30s)   61

FUNHOUSE (2)
Eric Bogosian (seriocomic/20s-40s)   65

GHOST ON FIRE (2)
Michael Weller (seriocomic/comic/30s-40s)   67

GLENGARRY GLEN ROSS
David Mamet (seriocomic/30s-40s)   69

HERRINGBONE
Tom Cone (seriocomic/20s-40s)   72

HUNTING COCKROACHES
Janusz Glowacki (seriocomic/30s-40s/Polish)   74

HURLYBURLY (3)
David Rabe (seriocomic/30s-40s)   75

THE INCREDIBLY FAMOUS WILLY RIVERS
Stephen Metcalfe (seriocomic/20s-30s)   79

IT'S ONLY A PLAY
Terrence McNally (comic/30s-40s)   80

THE JAIL DIARY OF ALBIE SACHS
David Edgar (serious/30s)   82

A KNIFE IN THE HEART
Susan Yankowitz (seriocomic/20s)   84

LES LIASONS DANGEREUSES
Christopher Hampton (seriocomic/30s-40s) 86

A LIE OF THE MIND (2)
Sam Shepard (seriocomic/20s-40s) 88

LYDIE BREEZE
John Guare (comic/30s) 91

MA RAINEY'S BLACK BOTTOM (2)
August Wilson (comic/60s/serious/30s/Black) 93

MARCO POLO SINGS A SOLO
John Guare (comic/30s) 96

THE MARRIAGE OF BETTE AND BOO (2)
Christopher Durang (comic/16/40s) 98

MOTEL CHRONICLES (2)
Sam Shepard (seriocomic/20s-40s) 100

MY DINNER WITH ANDRÉ (2)
Wallace Shawn & André Gregory (seriocomic/30s-40s) 102

NATIVE SPEECH
Eric Overmyer (seriocomic/30s) 105

THE NORMAL HEART (2)
Larry Kramer (serious/30s-40s) 107

ONE FOR THE ROAD
Harold Pinter (seriocomic/30s-50s) 110

OPEN ADMISSIONS
Shirley Lauro (serious/19-20s/Black) 111

ORPHANS (2)
Lyle Kessler (seriocomic/20s-40s) 112

A PIECE OF MONOLOGUE
Samuel Beckett (serious/20s-50s) 115

PLENTY
David Hare (serious/30s-40s) 116

PRAVDA
Howard Brenton & David Hare (seriocomic/40s) 117

A PRELUDE TO DEATH IN VENICE
Lee Breuer (seriocomic/20s-40s) 119

THE PROFESSIONAL FRENCHMAN
John Wellman (seriocomic/30s-40s) 121

THE REAL THING
Tom Stoppard (comic/30s-40s) 123

THE RESURRECTION OF LADY LESTER (2)
OyamO (seriocomic/30s/Black)   124

RIVKALA'S RING
Spalding Gray (seriocomic/30s)   127

ROAD
Jim Cartwright (serious/20s)   129

SAFE SEX
Harvey Fierstein (seriocomic/30s)   130

THE SEX ORGAN
John Quincy Long (comic/30s-40s)   133

SLAM!
Jane Willis (seriocomic/19-20s)   137

SWIMMING TO CAMBODIA
Spalding Gray (comic/30s)   139

TALLEY AND SON
Lanford Wilson (serious/20s)   140

TRACERS
John DiFusco (serious/19-20s)   141

WEST
Steven Berkoff (seriocomic/20s-30s)   143

WHEN I WAS A GIRL I USED TO SCREAM AND
SHOUT ... Sharman Macdonald (comic/16)   144

PLAY SOURCES   145

INTRODUCTION: ACTING SOLO

Where playwright and actor meet on the most matched and even of terms is in the monologue. The monologue is a shared moment between the playwright and his medium, the actor. It provides an opportunity for both artists to collaborate more directly than at any other stage of the theatrical process. With the monologue, the actor and playwright create a theatre of their own. Even the dialogue portions of a play are more collaborations between actor and actor, or actor and director. The playwright becomes a third or fourth party. But in the monologue the playwright depends entirely on the actor for clarity and precision. And for the actor, these gifts of extended thought and speech can be the key to liberation; points of separation that leave other actors in the play behind and propel the solo actor above everyone else in our estimation and concern. So totally are actor and playwright fused in the monologue, so completely intertwined, that the spirit and voice of one becomes indistinct from the other. The result can be that unique harmony rarely achieved on any stage.

The best theatrical monologues have a kind of thrust and propulsion that rivet our focus and attention. They grab an audience, stop time, and suddenly make the actor/character's plight the sole intention of the play. Good monologues leave behind the common language of the play and take on more exalted qualities. They take the speaker to a higher orbit of performance. When we speak of a Sam Shepard monologue, for instance, we frequently use the word "aria" (airs). In the theatre of the past, "hearing" and watching great actors grapple with and tame the language of great dramatists was the single reason for going to the theatre.

In a sense, monologues are exhibitions of writer's and actor's courage. They are blatant expressions of will, purpose, thought, feeling, rage, confusion, irony, hilarity, regret, defeat, and dozens of other human emotions. They are also egocentric in the extreme. A really fine monologue pinpoints a character's quirks and longings. Oftentimes it unleashes something raging inside the character. It may not, and should not, give a whole meaning to a play (only the *total* play can do that), but it can give luminous meaning to a single moment onstage. Just for a passing instance, maybe a minute or more, a character is given concentrated definition and content; perhaps more than we have yet experienced. Actors love monologues for their freedom and focus. They are showpieces and showstoppers. They jar us into understanding what a character has been straining to say. Often they are a test by which we can measure an actor. More often they separate the good writers from the bad. And after the play is said and done, monologues leave us with a memory of the event. Usually they contain the lines we most remember.

But just what is a monologue? Obviously it is a speech in which one person talks solo to himself, another character, or the audience. They provide the moments when the public spectacle of drama abruptly becomes personal and intimate. In the writing of a gifted playwright and the mouth of a daring performer, the monologue rises to the same plane as the operatic aria or any other tour de force of solo performance. It can also be as gutsy as a "rap" or bit of pop singing. But without the actor to give it release, the inner dynamic of a monologue remains uniformly contained and clumped on the page. Like music, every monologue is written like a score, with its own rhythms, beats, crescendos, and climaxes. And as with any sustained piece of showmanship onstage, monologues leave an unforgettable imprint on an audience when perfectly executed. We may not remember much about the dialogue in the scenes of Shakespeare's *Hamlet,* but we all remember details about how an actor performed any of the soliloquies that begin "To be or not to be," "O what a rogue and peasant slave am I," and "Now I am alone."

Contemporary monologues, like Shakespeare's great soliloquies, all have their roots in ancient song, odes, orations, and the extended speeches in Greek tragedy. That's how the form developed in the West. They equally find their source in prayer. Once the Greek actor Thespis stepped out of the chorus to deliver his speeches solo, the art of individual acting was born. And at that point, too, the actor's detachment from the background gave us something onstage to heighten our attention and curiosity.

Monologues are also playwright's tricks, providing actors with ingenious ways of attracting and holding our attention. They can also lead to moments of pure indulgence, or just be a pack of lies. Who said that a monologue has to tell the truth? Yet it is the actor's job to give the monologue a *sense of truth* or, at least, illustrate it

2

with a convincing performance strategy so that a constellation of words will do their trick and have their effect. Playwrights who love the sound of their own voices, Shaw for one, stud their plays with monologue after monologue. Most other playwrights use them more sparingly, and even tentatively, too frightened, perhaps, to hear their own voices or too certain that they will give away the essential meaning of their play. For monologues are confessions. They startle us with their candor, which is why they are so hard to do well. A character speaks urgently, and we, invariably, remember what he or she has said. And we remember it for a long time.

Just as they function like uninterrupted pieces of music or orations, monologues can also be like poems. They entrap a play's lyricism and challenge an actor in the skillful use of words and phrasing. Any decent monologue, just like any poem, can stand on its own as a piece of handsome writing. It still needs a speaker, though, to give it a final dimension. Yet monologues— contemporary ones, especially—can also be halting and stumbling; not things of great beauty at all. They can capture a character's inarticulateness as he or she strains to find the words, struggles to fill the void. Samuel Beckett writes only monologues nowadays to give his characters' obsessive thoughts free range onstage. Peppered with pauses, lapses, repetitions, and silences, contemporary monologues isolate the human inability to use words and make them meaningful. They hint at moments of modern experience where language no longer has the full expressive power and resonance to re-create the world in all its dimensions. Some monologues hope that a string of jangled phrases and "you know what I means?" will do the work of full thoughts and sentences. The speeches in David Rabe's *Hurlyburly* are severely stuck in this condition.

Monologues can also be excessively coarse and violently profane. They can catch an urban pulse that communicates largely through vulgarity. Some of the speeches of David Mamet and Eric Overmyer take us into a world of language that has a vicious core. In explosive pockets of the world, like South Africa, where discord is the rule rather than the exception, playwrights reproduce chaos and tension in the language of their rage. Even when the violence is more latent and fundamentally political and social, such British playwrights as David Hare, Howard Barker, Howard Brenton,

David Edgar, Jim Cartwright, and even Harold Pinter fight despair in monologues that characterize the personality and source of evil.

Monologues can also be highly physical as well as verbal. Some of the best have an intuitive feel for the way words can communicate through an actor's body as well as his voice. Steven Berkoff, for example, knows that actors speak to us *physically* as well as verbally; the body functions onstage in concert with the mind. And even more than male playwrights, women dramatists, like Nell Dunn, Sarah Daniels, Debbie Horsfield, Timberlake Wertenbaker, and Sharman Macdonald, can find the subject of their speeches in female physicality. The body, and thoughts of the body, can be uncommonly expressive. For the actor, these kinds of monologues can lead to rare moments of solo performance. Tom Stoppard's speeches show the actor that monologues can also be acrobatic, and that humor, at its very best, is physical and like a verbal pratfall. For some writers, words and sentences can be amorous, distilling, as Sam Shepard does in *Fool for Love* or Christopher Hampton does in *Les Liasons Dangereuses*, the intensity and jealously of sexual love.

During the past decade, the monologue has taken on new meaning and function. The well-crafted confessional speech, like those in the plays of August Wilson, are certainly still with us. But we seem to live more and more in a time where dialogue—really talking and listening *to* each other—is quickly being replaced by the monologue and a talking *at* one another. Wallace Shawn's plays, whether talking with André Gregory in *My Dinner with André,* or talking through the two women in *Aunt Dan and Lemon,* creates the effect of words being spewed at the audience. But we experience this all the time nowadays and are bombarded with examples of it daily: television chat shows, stand-up comics, tell-all autobiographies, political speeches, therapy sessions, protest rallies, advice manuals, T.V. evangelists, disc jockeys, voice overs, sales pitches, publicity spiels, rock videos, "rap" singing, and on and on. Someone is always telling us *their* side of the story rather than the *full* story itself. In fact, hardly anyone seems to know what the story is about anymore.

With the advent of "performance art" in the 1970s and a rebirth in old-fashioned storytelling, the solo performance piece and one-person show is now as common as it once was rare. Actors have always trotted out their anthology and "historical" character pieces (i.e., Mark Twain, Charles Dickens, Emily Dickinson, etc.) between other engagements. Now more actors—and younger performers not strictly classifiable as actors, like Laurie Anderson—are using the medium of the solo performance as the setting for a whole evening's work. In the case of Laurie Anderson, her spectacles are a combination of theatre, rock concert, and pop painting. For a performer like Lily Tomlin, the writer Jane Wagner's solo monologues walk a fine line between comic routine and single character dramatizations. In other cases the performer's own autobiography, as in the monologues of Spalding Gray, or observations of show business types and daily encounters with street people, such as the monologues of Eric Bogosian, become the stuff of solo theatre.

In a decade when great acting onstage has become a true rarity (a generality more true in the United States than in Great Britain), these different kinds of solo performance have now become serious factors in the acting process. Being *oneself* onstage as well as being a *character,* allows the actor a liberation that traditional theatre roles seldom provide. They encourage the actor to be more himself or herself, letting his or her voice penetrate the mask of acting. Since the teachings of Stanislavsky, the modern actor has been laboring hard to transform into someone else. Now both sides of the actor's self are on display. Analogously, reducing the human story to one's own words and gestures, traditionally the function of literature and writers, is now a territory open to anyone. The "new" performer can use his or her own words and not just those of a playwright. Solo acting gives the actor the freedom to truly make material his or her own and to reassert the will to take back possession of the stage.

YOUR SIXTY SECONDS OF FAME

Acting alone onstage, especially when faced with a crucial auditioning situation, is all too frequently talked about in terms of fear and terror. But let's look at it in the opposite way, as a kind of joy and exhilaration. Taking center stage puts you right at the heart of the theatrical experience. Rather than being at a disadvantage, you should feel the power of being in complete control. Unless the actor is totally at ease with the prospect of performing, how can you expect anyone watching you to take a keen and genuine interest in what you have to offer? The full enjoyment of acting is infectious and flows effortlessly from the stage out to the audience. This essential joy of performance, apart from the basic anxiety all of us feel at being singled out and "watched," really must be in place before you can attempt to do what follows. The *angst* of acting is the first obstacle you simply must clear from your path.

We assume that actors are looking at *Solo!* in the hope of finding fresh auditioning material, and maybe even some unexpected and new surprises from unfamiliar writers. But how you can best use this material onstage is what we want to explore with you.

Just by leafing through this book you're already accomplishing the first major step: choosing material. But let this choice be guided by something even more fundamental: choose material that best suits your capacity as a person as well as an actor. In other words, find a monologue that is close to you; not something that is close to the actor you would most like to be, but a piece of writing that reflects the actor you are now. In time, conditions will change as you change. But for the moment don't choose something old if you're young, don't toy with something flashy and "hip" if you're not. If you pick something British, for instance, be aware of the context and the *accent*. Are either of these out of your reach or your realm of experience? Many of the British pieces in *Solo!* present few obstacles or difficulties for American actors. We made sure of that in our selection process. Some can even be done with an "American" accent or by simply "translating" British words into American phrases. But remember that all writing, from whatever part of the world, has its own indigenous rhythms which only real familiarity can breed and make work. Honestly knowing your own capacity on this score can help you avoid a critical mistake when it comes to choosing a monologue.

Probably the best rule of thumb we can offer you here is to match your own personal sensibility with that of an individual playwright. Once you've made your choice, the monologue itself should immediately provoke you to search out its complete source, so that you can see and savour the speech in its full context as one part of a complete play. It's simply foolish for an actor to learn a monologue but be completely ignorant of the full text. There are really no shortcuts to good acting. What will you do, for instance, if a director begins asking you in-depth questions about your character or other moments in the play? Go about preparing your monologue just as you would a full role in a complete production. Now that you have one or several monologues in hand, let's plunge right into the deep of this section—the audition.

Auditions, no matter what anyone says, are often won or lost in the *first sixty seconds*. One minute is really all the time you have to truly establish a solid presence and make a definite claim on our attention. The first moment we lay eyes on an actor is rarely forgotten. That may sound prejudiced, but it is, in fact, true. And the sixty second countdown begins as soon as you enter the room, even before you speak your first line. Just your mere "presence" radiates an aura that the spoken monologue will only confirm or contradict. Yet in that first unspoken minute, it can often be "love" or "hate" at first sight. So begin now to think and learn how you can use these seconds to your full advantage.

Any audition is a performance. Make no mistake about that, even though we call them tryouts. And you can think of it as a performance—a solo performance—in which you are the star. The audition is also a very specialized kind of job interview in which you just don't answer questions but *perform* answers. But don't think of it as a contest with other actors. You are really competing with the clock and the short attention span of your auditors; especially short if they have seen a lot of other actors during the same audition. They want to be captivated by someone special, someone who likes the job of acting. Someone who is a professional and won't waste time. Unlike other job interviews, in an audition you rarely get the opportunity to repeat or retract what you just said or did the second

7

before. Those for whom you are performing (director, casting agents, drama school representatives) are clearly looking for talent. But they are also looking for a person with an appetite for work; someone who can become part of an ensemble and withstand the pressure of concentrated effort. Auditions are frequently tense because the eventual rehearsal process is even more intense. Show them, immediately, that you can bear the weight of an opening night performance. They are *not* looking for inadequacies, and they *will not* overlook flaws. But that's perfectly understandable. If they choose you for a part or place, so much time and energy will go into you. So they must get the clear impression from your audition that you can do the job better than anyone else. If you can master and break the sixty second barrier, you can be on the road to fame.

Getting through an audition in the correct frame of mind and with the right stuff requires a process you can repeat time and again. It should be a process no different from any other acting process you would use in rehearsal or performance. Here's one that seems to work best. It is a system that can be expanded to suit larger performance challenges or contracted to meet the concentrated needs of an audition. It incorporates *all* that is most useful from the many different techniques of actor preparation. And it distills what every actor—amateur or professional—needs to know in order to deliver an honest level of performance. Here are ten specific steps, linked in a chain, which can be quickly memorized in sixty seconds:

1. **PREPARATION**
2. **RELAXATION**
3. **CONCENTRATION**
4. **COMPENSATION**
5. **MOTIVATION**
6. **CHARACTERIZATION**
7. **PHYSICALIZATION**
8. **IMPROVISATION**
9. **REVELATION**
10. **RESOLUTION**

This chain contains all the fundamentals of good acting. It is not some magic chain of gold that will instantly turn you into a great performer. But, if you work through each step properly, it is a system that will not only get you through an audition but through an entire performance. We'll make general comments about each step in the process and then apply it more directly to the audition itself.

1. PREPARATION

No actor can work without being solidly prepared. And our approach here is to put you in the *highest* state of preparation. We'll begin by assuming that you have already chosen your material. Perhaps you've picked one classical monologue and one contemporary. But why not prepare a whole "audition repertoire" of different kinds of material? Being prepared means being able to shift gears from one kind of monologue and mood to another. As an actor you should strive to develop your range and not stay too confined within the narrowness of a couple of favorite pieces. Give your talent the opportunity to grow by experimenting with all kinds of pieces. You'll notice that *Solo!* is an expansive collection of the most varied kinds of monologues. That should be an indication of how we would like to encourage you to look at your acting, in broader terms while still remaining essentially yourself. Preparing a selection of monologues—perhaps six—means that you will never go stale. But proceed at a pace that will allow you to learn and know your material well.

Knowing your material means more than just learning the words and lines. Memorizing is not the challenge in this stage of preparation. Knowing indicates familiarity and intimacy with the play in all its parts. Really *read the play*. Not just once but several times. Investigate its background. Reveal its sources. Decipher its context and content. The best actors, even if just preparing for an audition, will read a script several times. Once you are performing the play, you never stop reading it. Carry the play with you, so that you can read it wherever you are. See it when other actors perform it. You'd better be curious about it because it is now part of your life as a performer. In other words, live and breathe the material. Let it grow on you. You, the character, and the whole play have now formed a partnership. Don't abuse the contract by learning only a single speech.

Further steps in this kind of preparation might be to experience ways that the monologue is written. A good trick is to write or type out the monologue as a means of experiencing the fusion of words and phrases. You might also write out new monologues for your character that the playwright has not written for his own play. The attempt here is to get deeper into the consciousness of the character and the writer. Unless the actor is willing to inhabit and discover the full life and world of his material, the acting of it will always seem false, uninformed, and, at its worst, dreadfully dull. Excite yourself by turning this stage of preparation into an adventure in which you unlock the secrets of the play and expose them.

Now start looking at your chosen speech in detail. What about it surprises you, moves you, makes you laugh? Humor is a powerful ally onstage. It can also be one of your most valuable assets in an audition. It breaks the ice and makes you appealing. Wit is a commodity that the best actors have in abundance. What about odd words and phrases? How can you handle them? What about the strong contrasts between words, the darkness and light that often inhabits the best speeches? Unless you can uncover the hope within the seeming hopelessness of a Beckett speech, for instance, the entire monologue will only result in something dead and dreary. Can you uncover the hope in the speech you've chosen, the way in which the monologue works towards some future success? Really *look* at the speech in order to unravel the playwright's intention so it becomes your character's intention. What are you trying to accomplish and convince us of in what you are saying? How does the monologue build in expectation and arrive at various plateaus or sudden bursts of recognition? All good speeches have some kind of "build," either upwards or downwards, towards a lively or still climax. Perhaps the speech has different kinds of motion. Maybe it rocks, sways, swaggers, stutters, falters, or trips. What does it *physically* feel like to you? Does it make you want to move and use your body in some special way? Then there is the ultimate personal test: Why do you *need* to say this particular speech and why say it now? Does it make you angry? Does it settle some personal score? Does it say something about you?

Long before entering an audition, the process of preparation begins with questions like these. They are the crucial questions that every actor must ask of a speech. So nail them down as you work on any piece of acting material. When you've satisfied yourself with some answers, you're ready to audition.

The audition itself: As we've already said, the audition is basically a job interview in which you act out your answers. It is *not* a life or death struggle in which your whole being and worth is being put to the test. If that was the case, how could you ever think of auditioning? Be a professional and think of the audition as a necessary stage in a professional process. Don't allow yourself to become incapacitated by something that should be enjoyable.

The best kind of preparation for any audition—apart from really knowing your material—is to begin with the thought that you *belong* at this audition. You are not wrong for the part nor are you out of place being here. All of your years of training and preparation have brought you to this point. And because we are approaching the audition not as a competition but as a race against the clock—overcoming the sixty second barrier—none of the usual feelings of embarrassment or inadequacy need to concern you now. Your objective it simply to work hard and get the job done; to show your acting personality to its full advantage in a short space of time. Believe that you will give the best performance of your career. Forget about the past or the future. The time you should be concerned with is only the present. So put all your energy and thought into this moment.

The preparation of any part—and a monologue should be approached as a part—is a highly technical procedure. Recall all the "given circumstances" and have them clearly before you. Key yourself to the moments just before the monologue begins. Who are you? What has just happened? Who are you talking to? In the time leading up to the audition, do a lot of work on the speech and character but then bury it and merge it into a seamless performance. All good acting demands freshness. It must appear as if it is happening for the first time. Think of the audition as your chance to give new birth to a character and speech. What you must strive for in an audition is *focus:* on the character, on the task, on the words. Become fixed and locked into a purpose. You are preparing yourself to launch into a speech because something *burning* needs to be said.

The image you project to others is doubly important when you enter any acting space. You are being judged on looks and bearing, as well as on the quality and delivery of material. Eyes are auditioning you as well as ears. So pay careful attention to the ways you prepare your dress and appearance. What you wear is crucial. Neutral dress might be the rule but coming on in more flamboyant clothes may be to your advantage. Think about the circumstances and particularities of each audition. Is the part sophisticated or "down and dirty"? Will your looks distract from the importance of what you are saying? Will red or black say something more about you than it says about the character? Costume yourself to meet the needs. Even your choice of shoes can say just as much as your monologue. Clothing has a way of speaking. Once you enter an auditioning space, the *total* you is on display. Leave nothing to chance or distraction. Prepare to look and be the part.

2. RELAXATION

No actor can hope to get the best, physically, from himself or herself without being in top condition. If you've been well trained in proper stage technique and physical work, you probably already know the best means to relaxation. The anxiety of an audition, the anxieties of life, produce tensions. They are the actor's greatest enemies. But muscular tension, especially around the neck and shoulders and in the voice, can be freed and relaxed through a proper physical warm-up. But begin it at home, working on all parts of the body. Adopt a good voice and speech warm-up, particularly if you are delivering a taxing speech or will be expected to sing. And always be prepared to sing. Carry a complicated poem with you to test your vowels and consonants, your sibilants and aspirants. If you have repeated difficulties with speech, seek out a good speech teacher. *How* we say things onstage is as important as *what* we say. Any relaxation techniques should really become part of your daily regimen. Once you get to an audition, you can quickly perform exercises that will tone you for the challenge ahead.

The audition itself: Arriving at an audition early, rather than just on time, can prove to be relaxing in and of itself. When you arrive out of breath, you arrive out of control. But set out from home assuming that the wait will be long and tedious. It usually is. Even assume that the room will be stuffy and claustrophobic. They usually are. Drink juice rather than stimulants in order to flush yourself out. Walk past the deli and donut shop. The taste of coffee or a

Coke will be that much better once the audition is over. Caffeine and sugar does strange things to us when we're already in a state of excitement. No alcohol and no drugs. Your mission is to be in complete control over all your functions. The mind needs to be composed and alert in order to give the best performance of your life.

Get an instant warm-up down to ten minutes or less. Some of this can even be done on the way to an audition; perhaps a brisk walk outside where you can talk or sing out loud without anyone paying too much attention. Always try to get out of transportation a few blocks away so that you don't have to plunge into the audition right off the street. Move at your own pace so that you can establish your own personal rhythm. And maintain it throughout the audition.

If the situation doesn't allow for a full warm-up, try doing one in your chair. Create a "state of relaxation" by visualizing the positive benefits of physical exercise: the movement of muscles, the circulation of the blood, the clearing of the head, the deep breathing. Listen and focus on sounds, smells, objects, and faces. In other words, center yourself. Do all you can to *separate* yourself from the tensions inside you. Take along something to read that will make you laugh. Don't listen to a Walkman if it will be just too distracting. Condition your passive self to begin shifting gears into an active mode. If you are just sitting there waiting, do some deep breathing: exhale the everyday self that is you and inhale the self that is you in the role. It's a simple technique. Part of your relaxation should be to find positive ways to fill the time until you are called. But relaxation also prepares you for the next crucial step of concentration.

3. CONCENTRATION

No one can tell you how to do this step easily. Each of us needs to acquire our own means of concentration. There are just too many ways—both practical and spiritual—of centering and focusing concentration on any given task. Being relaxed and conditioned is a good start. Emptying out the mind of its daily worries and strife, so that only the role and the monologue remains, is another good start. Rather than avoiding the task of auditioning, confront it. Make it a joy, an adventure. Maybe you will be "discovered" today. Maybe you will become famous. Since acting means *doing,* remember that there is nothing passive about it. It suggests conflict. So that might offer a good means of focus. Not the conflict and argument you may have had at home with a lover, but the character's conflict. All of your own fears and doubts can be centered on those of your character. So let the character absorb whatever outside conflict may be inhibiting you. Maybe the character wants to be as successful as you. Maybe he or she wants to be famous as well.

A positive way to begin concentrating on your way to an audition is to focus on a favorite play or film, reconstructing all the events in sequence, watching all your favorite actors going through their paces. Make yourself one of them. Become absorbed in your world, the world of the theatre. Many actors lose concentration on some level because the theatre is not special enough for them or because acting has lost its joy. We all spend too much time worrying about income and bills or the fame that eludes us and not enough time being concerned about the theatre. But once you drop these everyday concerns and begin concentrating on the great performances you've seen or been party to, you suddenly enter the best possible frame of mind for doing theatre. Now concentration turns into an eagerness to perform yourself.

The audition itself: Concentrate on turning fears into fixed purposes: getting prepared to enter the audition space, saying hello, and, most of all, readying yourself to say your first line. The opening of a speech is absolutely crucial. Here is where the clock really begins ticking away the seconds. It is the point of no return. The monologue itself begins to take over and take you along. Establish yourself in these first seconds. Root yourself onstage. Isolate the launch point in the speech and send it out to your listeners. Set-up your performance in advance. Mumble a bit of the speech outside the room before you enter. Let everything else evaporate as you begin concentrating on the character's needs and desires. Think of those first words as hot ignition points that will launch your whole performance into orbit. All of your acting will take-off from that cue.

Also use the time before entering the audition to dwell on motivation, the "whys" and "what ifs" of acting. Be concerned with making your performance new and *as if for the first time.* Even at this late stage of concentration, does anything suddenly surprise you about the speech? Rather than going over the monologue again and again to get the words right, work on it organically by concentrating on the events and circumstances leading up to the speech. Enter the room with energy and purpose. Enter it as a character with something important to say.

Also spend time concentrating on physical aspects and different means of unspoken communication. How can your eyes, head, neck, shoulders, arms, hands, fingers, hips, legs, and feet help with your acting a speech? Concentrate on getting the body to act with the mind in perfect harmony.

4. COMPENSATION

In acting, whether in auditions, rehearsals, or full performances, the unexpected can be a handicap. You must always be prepared to compensate for the things that go wrong. Your partner doesn't show up, the room is locked, your name's not on the list, it is cold, you are late leaving work or arriving. Compensate for all these disadvantages. Turn them into opportunities. The world is not perfect. Something always goes wrong. Compensate. Seek alternatives. Always be prepared, for instance, to sight read an unfamiliar script. Expect that the room for your audition will have shifted to some other place. Adapt to each change in plans. Compensate. The actor who can make adjustments onstage, in the very midst of a performance, is an actor who has learned the lesson of compensation.

The audition itself: Gauge the mood of an audition once you've arrived. Is the whole process running late? Is the atmosphere friendly or hostile? Be alert to the mood, not to gossip or other actors' fears, but to all the realities that might help you in your performance. Make sure that the space meets your needs. Are props there for you to use? Is there a sturdy table and chair? How resourceful will you need to be if none of these are available? Compensate for anything that is lacking. With the seconds ticking away, don't waste time searching for help. Size up difficulties in advance and maintain your control over the situation. Master any calamity. Do without something if you must. Allow yourself a well-defined but *constricted* acting circle. Don't expect to use the whole room. Never let events throw you off and distract you from your concentration. Keep apologies to yourself. Above all else, when things go wrong—and they will—don't make excuses. Simply adjust, compensate, and push ahead.

Adjust all your acting to the circumstances at hand. Don't pre-plan and pre-play a speech as if it will we done in duplicate conditions each time. Enjoy any variation that arises. Show that you are a resourceful actor who can perform anywhere. Your willingness to adjust and compensate adds dimension and range to your abilities as a performer. And your resourcefulness is certain to impress a director. This is exactly the kind of actor every director looks for.

5. MOTIVATION

Without doubt, motivation is the single most important link in this chain. Why? Because motivation gives directional focus to all acting onstage. Motivation gives us the *reasons* for doing and saying something through performance. It makes us perform an action or say a speech. Unless the actor knows *why* he or she sits in a specific chair, *why* we are talking to another character, *why* we are taking a drink, or *why* we are saying a speech, any task of acting will only be vague. Motivations provide us with answers.

Acting *without* motivation is dead-end acting. We come onstage to complete a series of choices we have already made in our mind. Motivation provides us with the reasoning and clarity of purpose to turn those choices into active responses. What can any actor *do,* what can any actor *say* with conviction unless backed by the push of motivation?

Motivation is the essential spring that triggers an actor into a scene, a role, a speech. Only after you have asked yourself the essential questions of acting—questions whose answers uncover motivation—can you begin to perform with authenticity: Who am I? What do I want? Where am I going? What obstacles stand in my way? Who am I talking to? What am I seeking or saying, beat by beat, word by word? Until the actor begins providing solid answers to these kinds of questions, acting will only be wasted energy. Point your acting in a specific direction.

The audition itself: Good motivation brings all the goals in a scene or speech together into one clear challenge. It gives the actor the *right* to claim the stage, even if it's just for the few precious

16

minutes that constitutes an auditioning monologue. Conviction comes from motivation. And your auditors will want to see you express conviction and belief from the first second you open your mouth. Once you have settled into your opening moment, you must let the *will, needs,* and *desires* of your character totally absorb you. Think of motivation as a replacement for self-consciousness. It is, after all, the consciousness of the character that should now be in control. The character's tasks and words now fill up the time. Your goals will be more easily accomplished if you have found the reason to be onstage.

Giving yourself even the slightest task to perform onstage has a way of obliterating self-consciousness. Walking across the stage trying to solve a mathematical problem puts you at more ease than just walking aimlessly across the room. The mind has nothing to focus on so it dwells on itself. For an audition monologue, isolate a *single* task that will give your acting the motivational push it needs. Find that one key activity that will give all the words clarity and purpose. Once absorbed in the activity, you'll barely even notice the time flying.

6. CHARACTERIZATION

Entering the world of a character is a lengthy and prolonged process. It means trying many different tacts before settling on the right one for you. The actor dives into the character repeatedly in the hope of penetrating all the layers. This is a rich process of discovery for the actor and is never arrived at instantly. You search the character's, as well as your own, personal history to find that equality that suits you both. And you never go public with this private work until a good part of the character's life and anatomy is in place.

For the purposes of an audition, entering a character's world begins from the moment you awake on audition day. How does he or she wash, choose clothes, dress, and groom for the day? What does he or she eat and drink? How do you begin shedding your own habits and take on those of your character? You *and* the character begin living and doing things together. Maybe you *both* choose to wear that red scarf or those brown shoes. Perhaps each of these pieces of dress give you important objects that will help you realize the character in performance. Perhaps you'll want to prepare your hair differently today. Will that help you get to the character? In other words, what will help you arrive at the audition *in character*?

The audition itself: When choosing audition monologues, you might try and search for pieces that demonstrate similarities. Can you, for instance, find something in Shakespeare's Ophelia that is like a character from a contemporary play? These don't have to be similarities that will make two monologues seem redundant, but parallels that are personal ones for you and help you transform from one piece to another while maintaining a strong and steady sense of character. The similarities might even be outrageous and secret ones. No one has to know except you. But transforming from a character in one monologue into that of another can be a peril. So why not try to find characters, or even speeches, that present you with some kind of harmony? You will be judged on your ability to fuse with a character. So your ability to believe in a character and make your audience share that belief is central to all acting. Simplify your audition task with a cast of sympathetic characters who are extensions of yourself. It will really pay off in the end and show in your performances.

The substance and shading that you give your characters will also be carefully noted. Perhaps you can find and add a different element to your role in each audition. Never be afraid to keep working on character. There is always something new to discover. This kind of process protects your characterization from becoming stale and lifeless. What new inflection can you add to a speech? What new turn on a phrase? Try to avoid too much consistency. It has a way of leeching the excitement out of a performance and can usually be detected. Always allow characters to keep surprising you. Treat the audition as you might treat any rehearsal: a new opportunity to go further with a character. But always keep one, solid aspect of character obvious and certain. Always have a strong baseline and never venture too far from it until you are ready.

7. PHYSICALIZATION

You suddenly find that you have a headache, the flu, or a fever. Can the way you feel today help serve your character? As you do your warm-up, you discover you can't rid yourself of a tightness in your chest. Can that be part of the character? The inner integrity of acting must align with how we feel physically. Never divorce one from the other. Any and all physical means must be explored as part of the process of building a role. The outer self is a rich resource that too many actors, especially in auditions, abandon. We rely too heavily on the words of a text. Remember that acting is something that has to be read from a distance. And our impression of an actor registers *externally* at first.

Acting is disciplined, hard work. It demands stamina along with mental concentration. It requires gesture as well as verbal agility. And the two must work in concert. The eyes, for instance, are remarkably important as instruments in a performance. How can they benefit you in your performance? Keeping your body alive and interesting onstage should receive as much work as the way you deliver a speech. If you are pliant, physically, a director will instantly see that he can work with you.

The audition itself: Don't just enter a room, enter it with interest. Make yourself the center of attention. Come in with a strong attitude and disposition. All of you is on trial. All of you is there to be read.

When delivering a monologue, what physical reactions do the words provoke? Too many actors forget to *move* with their words. And a speech that can physically show you off is usually the best kind to perform in an audition. Always pick a monologue that will make you perform an action. But also be careful about excessive gestures like flapping arms and hands that slice the air too much. Suit action to word, as Hamlet says to the players. Stay in control of each movement and gesture, letting the words lead you to a result rather than the other way around.

Voice and speech patterns are also aspects of the physical. Think about the cadence of your speech. Can you find a rhythm in the lines, even if they are not set in verse, that will give the words a musicality? Maybe you might even experiment with singing a monologue, or linking it with some form of music. The effort in an audition is to express a speech with impact. All stage language has · the capacity for lively expression. Words can be like objects tossed out to the audience. So projecting the words, as if they had solid weight, will enhance your delivery. Think, too, about the space in which you are performing. How much projection do you need to make your acting real? Project just to your auditors and not to a full house. Keep every aspect of your physicalization within proper bounds.

8. IMPROVISATION

Few actors improvise very well on their own. It takes enormous courage, daring, and self-regard to improvise with truth and conviction and then incorporate it into a full performance. Actors will too often hide behind a playwright's words rather than let their acting come out from behind the words. Yet we all admire creative risks onstage. Rehearsals usually offer ample time to experiment through improvisation. But what about within the confining limits of an audition?

The audition itself: Some auditions may ask you to improvise as a means of exploring your creative temperament. A director may want to explore different aspects of your capacity as an actor. An audition, for the brave, can be approached as an opportunity to take some sudden risks. A moment of improvisation, within the course of a monologue, may yield benefits. Most actors, however, will guard against going off the course of a routine once it has been set. Yet let yourself be taken by a creative impulse if it should suddenly happen.

Dull and consistent acting can hamper you. Our best acting ideas sometimes come to us in the heat of performance, once an audience has reacted to something we have just said or done. Here is a moment you can build upon. If you are in full control of yourself, your character, and your speech, you might think about enlarging on your performance in the midst of an audition. Any actor's job in these instances is to stand out and make an indelible impression. Literal interpretations of a speech have little to do with real acting. Theatricalizing yourself can be a real challenge. Avoiding the prosaic and the mundane can sometimes propel us to make these creative leaps. But do so only if the speech and your confidence naturally lends itself to this kind of risk.

9. REVELATION

Every good monologue contains a crucial moment when the whole speech reveals its intention. Find that moment so you can sustain it in performance. It may come at the beginning, middle, or end of the speech. A moment of revelation can be prepared for and scored. What, for instance, is the kernel of the speech, its most important word or phrase? Maybe it's the most important moment of the whole play. Such a revealed moment is something you can build a whole performance around.

The audition itself: Flatly delivered monologues, lacking a build, suggest flat acting. All dramatic language plunges us into a search for something. Yielding revealed moments in a monologue is really what an audition is all about. If you can transform an audition into a public search for something, that vital incident in the monologue, it will add impact to your task. Your concentration will increase, your physicalization will engage with the search, and your characterization will lock in place. You will also find yourself becoming one with the playwright's intention. Your struggle then becomes the center of our attention. That kind of involvement and discovery onstage is what your auditors will be looking for.

Find the right thread or through-line that will lead you to a revelation. Don't *rush* towards a result but *build* towards one. Use the words of the speech to heighten excitement and expectation. And when you make your discovery, make certain that it registers. Never smother the impact of a monologue's revelation. Sometimes they clearly stand out in a speech surrounded by pauses. They are there for the taking. Other times you have to work to find it. Revelations give speeches and performances the satisfaction of having arrived someplace important. Make sure that you can properly chart the path to one in your performance.

10. RESOLUTION

We all know that any kind of ending is hard to produce well. And any actor runs the risk of arriving at a result much too early. In monologues we have to give thought to how we end them and clearly signal that the performance is over and resolved. Any piece of acting is never over until there is a final curtain. Never just stop a performance. End it with finality and a conclusion.

The audition itself: Find the *curtain* in any monologue. Each speech has one. Is is fast or slow, a fadeout or a blackout? How long of a hold do you need? What is the best way to signal that you are through performing? Just as you build the opening of your audition carefully, so should you carefully prepare its conclusion. It can lead to success or ruin. The same rules for a fully staged performance apply to the audition. Letting the seconds of your ending subside, also gives you the moments to prepare for your next monologue. Your resolution lets you round off a performance. Perhaps more than any other part of acting, it shows your ability to control material and yourself. And throughout the minutes of an audition, control and completeness is what you strive to achieve.

ALBUM   David Rimmer

June 1965. A summer camp at night. BILLY *(16) sits flashing a flashlight, looking around.* HE *is tall, athletic and handsome and is dressed in summer clothes. With a pencil in hand,* HE *reads from a sheet of paper.* HE *is writing a letter to his friend,* MARSTON "BOO" PIERCY, *about the highs and lows of being a camp counselor. Different songs from an album by* THE BEACH BOYS *set off remembered events.*

BILLY: Dear Marston,
You incredible dipshit, what'm I doin' wastin' my time writin' a letter to you? Bein' a junior counsellor sucks. I hate tellin' kids what to do. They have to call me "Mister." I wake up in the mornin', they go, "Hey, Mister Buddwing, I wet my bed," and I think, "No, sorry, my father isn't here right now."
One cool thing. We had a party with the girl counsellors at this place Camp Idle Pines for Girls across the lake. We bought some beer. That's the other cool thing. The older guys go into town and get it for you. Anyway, I got some great action at that party. Y'know that album *The Beach Boys Today?* Cool album for parties. They put all the fast songs on the first side and all the slow songs on the second side, y'know, for dancin' and then makin' out. Really a cool idea. The Beatles oughtta do somethin' like that. Course it doesn't matter, everybody buys their records any-way—*(Crosses it out)*—God, who gives a shit about that?—So I end up with this girl Rita, and she's not exactly slutty or anything, but she's kinda fast. We're goin' at it, and they put on side two of the album. On "Please Let Me Wonder," we're dancin' close—very close; on "I'm So Young," squeezin' legs; on "Kiss Me Baby," lickin' ears; on "She Knows Me Too Well," swappin' spit; and by the time we hit "Way In The Back Of My Mind," my tongue was so Way In The Back of Her Head we didn't even *hear* the rest of the shit on the album! Woo! *(Fearing* HE'S *too loud,* HE *looks*

23

around, flashing the flashlight) So that's how it is up here, you turd-ball, 'cept I'm lyin' just a little to show you how cool I am. Aaah, I'm wastin' my time. You stupid asshole, what the hell you doin' goin' away to school way up in the goddamn woods? Go ahead, I'm not gonna stop ya, whadda I care, I'm not gonna miss ya, that ain't cool. Get on up there. See ya sometime.

Sincerely yours, you dipshit,
Signed, Billy Bones
P.S. Have a good life

(Beat)
What a bunch of shit. *(Crumples the paper, throws it down.)*

AMADEUS   Peter Shaffer

18th-Century Vienna. SALIERI, a middle-aged court composer, suffers from an intense jealousy for the young prodigy MOZART. HE finds one of MOZART's manuscripts (Symphony #29 in A Major). Reading it and then gradually hearing the perfection of the music, SALIERI is overwhelmed by the blatant proof of MOZART's genius. HE drops the manuscript pages and falls senseless to the ground. Finally the clock strikes nine and SALIERI stirs. Slowly HE raises HIS head and looks up. And now—quietly at first—HE addresses HIS God.

SALIERI: *Capisco!* I know my fate. Now for the first time I feel my emptiness as Adam felt his nakedness . . . *(Slowly HE rises to his feet)* Tonight at an inn somewhere in this city stands a giggling child who can put on paper, without actually setting down his billiard cue, casual notes which turn my most considered ones into lifeless scratches. *Grazie Signore!* You gave me the desire to serve you—which most men do not have—then saw to it the service was shameful in the ears of the server. *Grazie!* You gave me the desire to praise you—which most do not feel—then made me mute. *Gra-*

zie tanti! You put into me perception of the Incomparable— which most men never know!—then ensured that I would know myself forever mediocre. *(His voice gains power.) Why? ... What is my fault? ...* Until this day I have pursued virtue with rigour. I have labored long hours to relieve my fellow men. I have worked and worked the talent you allowed me. *(Calling up) You know how hard I've worked!*—Solely that in the end, in the practice of the art which alone makes the world comprehensible to me, I might hear Your Voice! And now I do hear it—and it says only one name: Mozart! ... Spiteful, sniggering, conceited, infantine Mozart!— who has never worked one minute to help another man!—shit-talking Mozart with his botty-smacking wife!—*him* you have chosen to be your sole conduct! And *my* only reward—my sublime privilege—is to be the sole man alive in this time who shall clearly recognise your Incarnation! *(Savagely) Grazie e grazie anchora!* *(Pause)* So be it! From this time we are enemies, You and I! I'll not accept it from You—*Do you hear? ...* They say God is not mocked. I tell you, *Man* is not mocked! ... *I* am not mocked! ... They say the spirit bloweth where it listeth: I tell you No! It must list to virtue or not blow at all! *(Yelling) Dio Ingiusto!*—You are the Enemy! I name Thee now—*Nemico Eterno!* And this I swear. To my last breath I shall *block* you on earth, as far as I am able! *(He glares up at God) (To Audience)* What use, after all, is Man, if not to teach God His lessons?

THE AMERICAN CLOCK   Arthur Miller

The present. ARTHUR ROBERTSON *(60s-70s), a corporate leader, looks back on the 1930s and the disastrous effects of the Great Depression. Both parts of the monologue come at separate points in the play, but each are about the same events.*

(ROBERTSON appears—once again an old gray-haired man with a serious grin.)

ROBERTSON: By my twenty-fourth birthday I had a seven-figure income; I considered retiring at twenty-eight. I've been a little of everything—war correspondent, ad-man, engineer—we built a section of the Sixth Avenue subway, in fact—I've worked in many countries, but I guess the most shocking thing I ever saw was from the window of my Riverside Drive apartment. It was like Calcutta, thousands of people living in cardboard boxes, tin shanties along the Hudson River right below the Drive—at night their campfires flickered right down the length of Manhattan Island, like an army encampment. Some nights I'd go down and walk among them; remarkable, the humor they still had, and of course people still blamed themselves rather than the government. But there's never been a society that hasn't had a clock running on it and you couldn't help wondering—how long? How long would they stand for this? There were nights you could almost hear it in the air ... (HE *clucks his tongue like a clock, glaring out, continuing until ...*) [CURTAIN ACT I]

* * *

ROBERTSON: I did a lot of walking in those days. The contrasts were so startling. Along the West side of Manhattan you had eight or ten of the world's greatest ocean liners tied up—I recall the S.S. Manhattan, the Berengaria, the United States—most of them would never sail again. But at the same time they were putting up the Empire State Building, highest in the world. But who would ever rent space in it when there were whole streets and avenues of empty stores? It was incredible to me how long it was lasting. I would never, never have believed we could not recover before this. Whole years were passing, a whole generation was withering in the best years of its life . . . *(The light on him goes out.)*

ASINAMALI! Mbongeni Ngema

The present. Leeuwkop Prison, outside Johannesburg, South Africa. A group of blacks, imprisoned under martial law, tell stories to each other about life on the outside. SOLOMZI BISHOLO *(20s) is a con man and pickpocket who practices HIS trade on unsuspecting victims at mass funerals and demonstrations.* HE *tells the others about the exploits of the notorious* BRA TONY *(Brother Anthony). The monologue is continued at different points in the play.*

SOLOMZI: *(Moves downstage)* I come from Soweto. I never really got involved with politics, I got involved with Brother Anthony *(Says it with admiration)*, we called him "Bra Tony." Heh, heh, heh *(Laughs)*. Bra Tony, he was a good man. Brilliant pickpockteter. Very intelligent. He knew exactly where the money was in a man's body. He understood a man's body very well. Haaa Bra Tony, he was like Dr. Chris Barnard. [. . .] I want to tell you something. Robbing and stealing, beautiful job. Especially if you work with guys like, Bra Tony! Ha ha ha! *(Laughs)* Bra Tony, he was a good man, a very close friend of mine. We were always together, just like twins. Hey man, that guy, he was always very neat. Ten gallon Stetson hat on top. China eyes sunglasses like those of Ray Charles or Stevie Wonder. Double-breasted Jacket. Pants? Brooks Brothers. Down below Florsheim shoes. A very thin belt, he used to call it a lizard skin. Beverly Hills Shirt straight from the U.S.A.! Ahahahaha! Bra Tony, he was a good man. A big name in robbery. All newspapers got his name. *Johannesburg Star* extra headlines: "Bra Tony." *Cape Times, London Times, New York Times, Radio Zulu, Radio Freedom.* John Voster Square police headquarters: "Watch out for Bra Tony!" Brixton Murder and Robbery Squad files: "Bra Tony!" Johannesburg Stock Exchange: "Watch out for Bra Tony!" South African Defence Force, Army and Navy: Bra Tony! Bra Tony Bra Tony! Jaaaa Bra Tony, he was a superstar. Do you remember that greatest train robbery in Johannesburg that hit international headlines. That was us. Do you remember that greatest train robbery in Johannesburg that hit international headlines. That was us. Do you still remember that airplane that was robbed in the Transkei airport in 1976. Operation Prime Minister Matanzima's Private Flight! That was us. 1977, Putco bus robbery, Durban, 1979 Ford Motors, Johannesburg. 1980 Coca Cola Industries, Durban, the very same year Operation Underground Backlys Bank, Krugersdorp. 1981 Zimbabwe Embassy, Operation Immigration. Where were you in 1982, Holiday Inn, Johannesburg Airport. 1983, IBM wage office, payday. 1984, Shabalala Incident, Soweto. [. . .] Ja Bra Tony, he was a good man. A very close friend of mine. I remember this Indian woman we met at Verulem Station, a small railway station miles away from Durban City. It was a very dull day for Bra Tony and myself. We found this woman in the waiting room at about 9:30. She was waiting for a train from Durban to Zululand. Majita! [Guys!] She was very pretty. We started chatting and within a short space of time we had become friends. She started telling me that she had resigned from her job. That woman was beautiful. You know that feeling when you see a pretty woman! I tell you, that woman was divine! We started touching fingers. My God. I don't know how Bra Tony got to know that she had money. He stood up, pulled out his big knife. She was looking at me, pretty thing man, in shock. She trusted me. Bra Tony just *(Slaps!)* slapped her so hard that saw tears flying out. Bra Tony said; "The

28

money!" and she said; "I . . . I . . . I have no money." Bra Tony repeated that action. He hit her face again. The stomach. The back. The head, the bottom. Her skirts were flying in the air. When she turned around to look at him, Bra Tony was there. He looked at her. Directly in her eyes. "Give me your panties." She said; "I . . . I . . . I'm having my period." "My baby, sweetheart, give it to me." You know what she did? She pulled down her panties and Bra Tony grabbed the whole thing. A big roll of money came out man.

(The other prisoners snore loudly. SOLOMZI *notices and turns around to face them)*

Nilele, minqundu yenu. Ndithetha ndodwa ngathi ndisibhanxa. [You bastards are asleep. I end up talking to myself as though I was crazy.] Ha . . . Bra Tony *(HE joins them and lies down)* Bra Tony, Bra Tony *(In a voice that fades with sleep.)*

AS IS   William M. Hoffman

The present. A New York City apartment. SAUL *(30s) and* RICH *(30s), former lovers, are splitting up and have met to divide their belongings. The tension between them mounts.* RICH *gets angry and is about to leave.* SAUL *stops him to finally tell about the death of some friends from AIDS.*

SAUL: Don't go. Please. *(RICH sits. There is a long pause)* I visited Teddy today at St. Vincent's. It's very depressing . . . He's lying there in bed, out of it. He's been out of it since the time we saw him. He's not in any pain, snorting his imaginary cocaine, doing his poppers. Sometimes he's washing his mother's floor, and he's speaking to her in Spanish. Sometimes he's having sex. You can see him having sex right in front of you. He doesn't even know you're there. *(Pause. Both men look down at their feet)*

Jimmy died, as you must have heard. I went out to San Francisco to be with him the last few weeks. You must have heard that, too. He was in a coma for a month. Everybody wanted to pull the plug, but they were afraid of legal complications. I held his hand. He couldn't talk, but I could see his eyelids flutter. I swear he knew I was with him. *(Pause)*

Harry has K.S., and Matt has the swollen glands. He went in for tests today . . . I haven't slept well for weeks. Every morning I examine my body for swellings, marks. I'm terrified of every pimple, every rash. If I cough I think of Teddy. I wish he would die. He *is* dead. He might as well be. Why can't he die? I feel the disease closing in on me. All my activities are life and death. Keep up my Blue Cross. Up my reps. Eat my vegetables.

Sometimes I'm so scared I go back on my resolutions: I drink too much, and I smoke a joint, and I find myself at the bars and clubs, where I stand around and watch. They remind me of accounts of Europe during the Black Plague: coupling in the dark, dancing till you drop. The New Wave is the corpse look. I'm very frightened and I miss you. Say something, damn it.

(Beat.)

AZTEC   John O'Keefe

The present. An open stage with a simple table and chair. A middle-aged MAN, nameless, is sitting at the table, HIS conversation already in progress. This is the opening section of a longer, full-length monologue.   It is a contemplation on the identity of an anonymous skull.

MAN:
Well, he got this skull off this gang of goons, you know. Motorcycle types. It was perched up on the forks of a Harley with a little Nazi helmet on it and everything. And this guy, he was a coroner or something, he asked if he could buy it. And after they pushed him

around a bit, this big guy let him have it for fifty bucks, the skull, you know.

It wasn't scary. It was just . . . a thing.

Well, this coroner took it to a forensic sculptress and she took measurements of it, nasal aperture, projection of the nose, temples, set of the jaw, setting up, smearing skin over it, in clay, you know. And you know what? She made a face out of that thing. I mean it didn't happen all at once, it went through stages. At first it looked like a rotten corpse, the kind you see in horror comics, and then it looked like this, this, incredible hooded skull man. So wise, so deep with black, hollow, endless eyes, eyes so deep you could only see the blackness. And the clay on the temples made the skull look like it was growing its own cowl.

And then it became human. I don't know when it exactly happened, what piece tipped it over the edge. It was just before the eyeballs were set in. Something about the way the cheeks flowed into the chin. But maybe it was the eyebrows, you know, that shape like cavemen moving through time. And then she put black hair on it. It was just a guess, I suppose, just a guess, but it made it, it really made it . . . a black-haired man. It was a black-haired man. He looked like he was thinking. He looked so intelligent, like he knew something. Like a rock would think if it could be a man.

Well, I don't know what happened to it. It just went away like you know when things close up. It's somewhere, probably on the shelf of some precinct somewhere.

Bones last a long time. Did you know that aluminum last forever? Longer than a pickled fish. A pickled fish only lasts six months.

I guess they figured out who the guy was. Killed himself. Couldn't leave his family conscious. Felt bad, not mad, just bad. Bad, like on the other end of something or like a hole got cut in the middle of it. Don't know how he died. No marks. Maybe asphyxiation, dehydration, starvation, wandering in the desert. They found him in the desert. Looked like he had been there a long time. Wasn't a white man. Probably Indian, Mongoloid you know. About twenty or so, bad teeth, no dental work. Thought he had killed himself. Maybe not though, maybe just wandered around drunk in the desert after a card game in some little desert town. I mean, the skull wasn't that old, maybe fifteen, twenty years back. That would be when gas was cheaper, things different, not so sad. Or, maybe just lost his car. You know, how those Indians drive. Could I have some water?

BATTERY   Daniel Therriault

The present. "Rip's Electric" shop. RIP (late 20s) enters, bursting with vibrant energy, and begins telling HIS assistant, STAN, about HIS score last night with an unnamed woman. The high performance power in the speech is totally in keeping with RIP's name and profession. This monologue has been adapted from the original source.

RIP: The night was a fight, a sad sight was my plight, but I gained height like a kite, when I plugged tight with my might! [...] I caught her in my sights at ten o'clock last night at Fatrack's Bar. Took aim at the target, tugged at the trigger, and fired at her with a sloe gin fizz. Shot up myself with a shooter. The bartender hit her with the bullet. I made my mark. I was sitting next to her. In like Flynn. [...] Perfection. Fresh off the assembly line. Her chrome shone. Fire-engine redhead. Not a dent in her fenders. Not a scratch on her doors. Her exhaust was sweet, pure premium. I was gettin' high from the smell of her gasoline. And she was soooo young. *(STAN begins to interrupt)* You want me to tell the story? *(STAN says, "Yeah")* Then let me tell the story. Alright? [...] Alright. *(Pause)* So I'm revving like a tuned engine in neutral, right? I grease her with another sloe gin. I'm gettin' oiled

32

with my own shots. What does she say? [...] She looks at me dreamy-like and says, "Your eyes are deep and clear as a Minnesota lake. I want to take off all my clothes and skinny-dip in them." [...] In my eyes. No clothes. [...] She said that. Where's my coffee? *(Pause)* I cruise over to her place. My wheels, her pad. Right? [...] Rule number one: When humping a bumper? Pump your brains out. Rule number two: Plug's pulled, light's out. You make your getaway. If you stay with a woman after making love, it's like flooding your engine. You must maintain. Plug's pulled, you leave. [...] A woman is like your key to the ignition. You stick her in the drive shaft, she cranks the motor, gets you where you're going, then you put her in your pocket 'til next time. [...] So where was I? Her place. *[Building excitement]* Billows of pillows. She was a natural red-head, you know what I mean? Hundred percent Irish, believe me. She sparkled like Waterford crystal. I took out my dipstick to precheck. She was oozing with oil. We were in park at the head of the strip. I twisted her starter. We kicked over into a steady uphill climb in low. I fit like she was custom made. When the rhythm was right, I threw her into first. We took off like two T-birds dragging down a dirt road. Pumping pistons. Supercharged eight-cylinder. Threw it into second. She was in spasms. Forced it into third. She blew my circuit. I flipped her over into reverse. We smoked. Bolted like a bitch. One goddamned greased engine. All jets blasting. To the bone. Busting the sound barrier. To the wire. My face pressurized into contortions. Two gees, five gees, nine gees. We began fishtailing. Her hips double-jointed. A spiritual experience. The Ascension. Flailing tongues of fire. A litany to saints. The finish line. The flag went down. First place. I grabbed the trophy! *(Calming)* Afterward I cooled my jets. Tried to regulate my breath. She purred in idle. She even smelled like burnt rubber. [...] Energy. I rolled onto the floor. She was stuttering and mumbling, trying to form the words "thank you," but her

33

lips were too spent. Like an angel, she slowly descended to Earth wrapped in swirling clouds of sheets. I said, "Hey baby, you deserve it," and disappeared. [. . .] Her name? *(Incredulously)* Her name? Who cares what her name was? *(Boastingly)* But I bet she remembers my name 'til she dies. Rip. 'Cause I ripped her to pieces. Aces. *(Pause)* So what did you do last night? Pull pud?

BODIES   James Saunders

The present. A suburban living room in London. MERVYN *(40s), an English schoolmaster, "approaching the evening of his life," recounts an affair* HE *had several years before with* HELEN, *the wife of his friend* DAVID. MERVYN *recaptures the start of the affair in several first act monologues. The thrill of the affair is eventually compromised when* HIS *wife,* ANNA, *discovers it.*

MERVYN: I don't know when it started. I'd always assumed she was an attractive woman—most women are—but I'd never *noticed* she was. I began to remember details about her, the way a painter would, the shape of the fingernails, the colour of the eyes, the way she held her head, and the details had a kind of value, as they would to a painter. I'm not observant, I've always dreaded witnessing a crime, seeing the robbers leave the bank, being asked by the police: what exactly happened, what time was it, what did the man look like, was he wearing a hat, was he clean-shaven, is this him? So it was unusual, how she came into focus; I could have painted her from memory—if I could paint. Then I found I enjoyed talking to her, just me with just her, without the usual worry: am I boring you, do you really want to be talking to me? She listened, listened very intently, watching my mouth, letting me talk, hanging on my lips you might say, it was very pleasing. I found I was flirting with her; she was an old friend, the others were always there, it was an unspoken joke between us, no harm in it . . . One night we were

34

coming back from the theatre, the four of us, in my car. Anne was in the back with David, Helen in front with me. I could hear them talking behind me, about the play, about theatre. Helen was quiet. I had a feeling I'd had before, of something passing between us; something was being said. She lit me a cigarette, put it in my mouth, her fingers touched my lip for a moment. The silence went on, while the others chattered in the back. I flashed a look at her face; she was watching my hand on the wheel, very intently. That's when I realized that she—desired me, and I her, and that we both knew; that the way was open. The tension was extraordinary. I changed gear, and left my hand there as if casually, the back of the hand brushing her skirt.

* * *

MERVYN: Back of the hand barely touching the skirt. God, I thought, they must feel it back there, the waves of it, like bloody D-Day! After that it was torment. Of course it was totally impossible: her best friend, the wife of my best friend; we lived practically in each other's pockets. It was mad. I tried to rationalize it away. I said: it's obvious what's happened. She's rather fallen for me for some reason, after all this time, perhaps they're having trouble; she's dissatisfied, looking around for something else. But that's her business. I don't have to follow suit. I'm flattered, that's all it is, because she wants me at a time when I don't feel particularly wanted. Don't be a fool, don't behave like a child. Keep clear. Forget it. It'll go away. I knew the cost of it, I was no beginner: the sick excitement, the lurchings, the constant planning, the tearing in two; a few islands of extraordinary happiness in a waste of messy discomfort. I've wondered since whether I could have stood out against it. I don't know, I suppose I could, I was a rational human being, part of me anyway. The letting go is always a conscious decision, whatever they say. What tipped the balance, as before, as always, was first, an anger. How dare things be this way! That the

35

simple, good coming together of two people is made an act of madness! Then a fear. I was afraid of losing something of myself, afraid, in a way, of dying. The need, the desire, whatever it was, was *my* experience; it was real, however painful it was, however perverse, it was mine, it was me, it was the only real thing about me, that awful obsessive clawing, the clawing of that need to be myself, to do what needed to be done if I were not to kill part of myself by killing that need. So I did it; or it was done. One day I let go.

* * *

MERVYN: Came the time when I realized Anne knew; and a new ritual set in. Having to make excuses for absence, knowing they weren't believed: "Stopped for a drink on the way, met so-and-so"—knowing she knew I lied. But the game had to be played out. "Oh, how is he? What did he say?" "Fine, I think. Nothing of interest. Sends his regards." She knew; I knew she knew; she knew I knew she knew. We played the game, terrified of what would happen if it came into the open. And taking it with me when I went to see her—Helen. Taking, I mean, Anne's—suffering. I tried not to call it that, but there was no other word for it. Suffering. Her suffering which I caused. Did I stop? No; I went on: more, it drove me from the house, I tried to escape from it, if it was only for an hour or two. Made love to *her,* and it was beautiful, beautiful. And all the time, *her* suffering, inside me, clawing. Till it broke.

THE BODY   Nick Darke

Early morning. A bright summer's day outside the fence of an American missile base in the English countryside. A dead MARINE *is discovered, sits up and begins telling this story to the audience. The circumstance of* HIS *death is not immediately clear.* HE *tells about being transformed into a fighting machine.*

BODY: I'd like to tell y'all a story. But before I begin, we have to go back, to the beginning when I was alive, towards the end of my life—by the way I'm dead right now. I died, close on five minutes ago—I had a fear of yawning. Got to figuring if I yawned too hard the skin round my lips, when they opened wide, would peel right back over my head and down my neck and turn me inside out. I started to yawn when I was sixteen, back home, when I was bored. I know that healthy guys when they hit sixteen start to do things other than yawn. But believe me where I came from there was little hope of that. And yawning was the next best thing. One day my paw caught me yawning. He said, "Son, join the marines." I said, "Paw, I'm bored." He said, "That marines will sure kick the shit outa that." So I enlisted. First thing they do is cut my hair off. Which kinda makes me uneasy 'cus by now I'd reached neurosis point about this skin peeling business, and I figured the only thing which would stop the skin from shooting right back over the top of my skull when I yawned was the hair. Figured it might like hold it in check long enough for me to yank it all back into place. But on my first day . . . had my head shaved . . . believe me I kept my mouth tight shut. But, by the end of my training at boot camp on Parris Island I was a highly-tuned killing machine, prepared to be sent to any part of the world, get shot up and die protecting the free world from the onslaught of Communism. Paw was right. Sure kicked the shit outa yawning. I was ready to kill. Go over the top. I had a weapon in my hand and my finger itched to squeeze the trigger. Got to figure if it itched much more it'd drop off. I had visions

37

of me, under fire, storming a tree line in a fire fight and comin' up face to face with a big Soviet stormtrooper and there I am weapon in hand ready to blast the bastard to boot hill finger on the trigger and the damn thin's itchin' so much it drops off. We were issued with ointment anyhow to relieve the . . . er, but, what happens? I'm sent here. Guarding warheads. Sitting on top of that observation tower, which thank Christ was made unsafe by the last gale, and walking up and down the fence, guarding warheads against sheep! I started yawning again. Twice, three times a day. Then it hit me. We were trained to kill, and to die. Now I dunno whether any a you good people are dead, but if you are still alive, the one thing that bothers us about dying is what happens after. I only died five minutes ago but it strikes me being dead is much the same as being alive. It's boring. I think I've bin sent to hell. Don't die. I made a mistake. I erred. It's hell all right. So. I'm dead. And in hell. (HE *lies down again. Dead.*)

BOPHA!*　　　　　　　　　　　Percy Mtwa

The present. A black township in South Africa. ZWELAKHE (20s), a radical black student and son of a policeman, gets caught-up in a violent street protest and is arrested. HE gives some vivid impressions of what it was like.

ZWELAKHE: Policemen were advancing the fighting, the destruction, the shooting bullets breaking windows above you, dogs barking, the running, the ducking, the falling, the screaming, the panic, the fear, and the dying, and this was only a funeral of our Comrade Pule Rampa, who died in detention held under the state of Emergency. Why don't people know when to stop. Ngudle died in Pretoria, suicide by hanging. Modipane died in Prison—slipped in

---

* *Bopha!* is Zulu for *"Arrest."*

38

the shower. Timol died in Johannesburg, fell from the tenth floor window during interrogation. Biko died in Pretoria, injured in a scuffle. Many unknown people died on unknown dates in unnamed prisons no details given. We take it easy and bury our dead, and I'm telling you gents, there is never any violence until the police come. These people are killing us. Many people lay scattered in the streets, many were injured, many were dying, and many were dead. I saw a black policeman kick a young boy in the face, a boy who was shot and almost bleeding to death, and he said we school children are giving them overtime. Another white policeman was laughing at a man who was rolling on the ground in terrible pains and he said he was doing break dance. People were hiding in their houses and in the back-yards waiting. Suddenly I heard voices singing from far-away. People were coming back, the whistling, the shouting, *"SIYAYI NYOVA."* Everybody came out and charged into the streets. One two three the whole township was in flames—Putco buses, delivery trucks, company cars, hippos, police vans, houses, shops, and people. The township was also filled with smoke from burning people. Mayors, community councilors, informers and black policemen.

I saw a small boy pick up a stick, with it he shoved pieces of human flesh back into the fire, a policeman burning to ashes, with tears in his eyes said the police killed his mother. Policemen killing people and people killing policemen *wafa-wafa* [die-die]. Policemen were waiting outside the church with guns, and also waiting outside the church with a gun was my father. He knew I was inside the Church. And I was singing.

BORDERLINE   Hanif Kureishi

The present. An Asian community in West London. HAROON
*(19), a bright Indian student and writer, wants desperately to escape
the narrow confines of a segregated life.* HE *tells his girlfriend,*
AMINA, *about* HIS *hopes to break free, building them around the
story of a house burglary.*

HAROON: You know, when we were kids, my brother and I
were taken to people's houses. Dressed up and everything. Like
being wrapped in brown paper. We just about creaked. In the
houses we visit everything's on exhibition: furniture, their wife's
hair, their kids, their kids' teeth. You've got to admire everything.
They have to admire you, your teeth, hair, shoes. Everything seems
to smell of perfume. You can't touch anything. My brother says he
has to piss. He's in their hall. I know he's going through their
pockets in the hall. I know he's opening their handbags. They're
asking me how I'm doing at school. I'm saying I'm doing well. I
can hear fivers settling in his pocket. I can hear my father saying,
"answer them, Haroon, they're our friends." I can hear myself
saying, "I'm good at *Engish*." That Sunday he steals a car. It's a
Jag. I'm lying on the backseat. We're on the by-pass. We're doing 60. We're doing 90. We're going out to Greenford. I'm completely numb. They're in a house in Greenford. I'm outside. I can
hear him and his friends moving across thick carpets, unplugging
speakers, lifting down TV sets. I'm looking out. Soon I'm not
looking out. In fact I'm running away. I'm away. They're walking down the drive with a spin-dryer. I'm not there. Two men are
running towards them. They're arresting them. My father's curs-
ing. My mother's hysterical. I'm locked in my room. I'm studying, I'm protected, I'm the special son, the hope, my brain's burning . . . *(Pause)* Everyone round here's too busy serving kebabs
and learning karate! No one round here knows fuck-all about what
you want to know about.

[AMINA: At least we protect each other here.]

HAROON: We've got to engage in the political process. Not just put out fires when they start them. Yasmin and Anwar—they're brave. But they're separatist. I say we've got to get educated. Get educated and get inside things. The worm in the body, Amina.

BRIGHTON BEACH MEMOIRS   Neil Simon

1930s. A house in Brighton Beach, Brooklyn. EUGENE *(16) is lying on* HIS *bed, making another entry in* HIS *"memoirs." This one concerns a conversation between* HIS *mother,* KATE, *and his aunt,* BLANCHE, *about a dreaded disease. All of* EUGENE's *monologues are directly to the audience.*

EUGENE: *(Writing, says aloud)* "That's-what-they-have-gutters-for" . . . *(To audience)* If my mother knew I was writing all this down, she would stuff me like one of her chickens . . . I'd better explain what she meant by Aunt Blanche's "situation" . . . You see, her husband, Uncle Dave, died six years ago from . . . *(He looks around)* . . . this thing . . . They never say the word. They always whisper it. It was—*(He whispers)*—Cancer! . . . I think they're afraid if they said it out loud, God would say, "I HEARD THAT! YOU SAID THE DREAD DISEASE! *(He points finger down)* JUST FOR THAT, I SMITE YOU DOWN WITH IT!!" . . . There are some things that grown-ups just won't discuss . . . For example, my grandfather. He died from—*(He whispers)*—Diptheria! . . . Anyway, after Uncle Dave died, he left Aunt Blanche with no money. Not even insurance . . . And she couldn't support herself because she has—*(He whispers)* Asthma . . . So my big-hearted mother insisted we take her and her kids in to live with us. So they broke up our room into two small rooms and me and my brother Stan live on this side, and Laurie and her sister Nora live on the other side. My father thought it would

41

just be temporary but it's been three and a half years so far and I think because of Aunt Blanche's situation, my father is developing—*(He whispers)*—High blood pressure!

CHILDREN OF A LESSER GOD   Mark Medoff

The present. The scenes of the play take place in the mid of JAMES LEEDS *(30s), a speech teacher at a state school for the deaf.* JAMES *has married* SARAH NORMAN, *who is totally deaf and who also wants to be a teacher. During a climactic argument between them* JAMES' *anger brings* SARAH *to the point of actually speaking.*

JAMES: Yeah? You think I'm going to let you change my children into people like you who so cleverly see vanity and cowardice as pride? You're going nowhere, you're achieving nothing, you're changing nothing until you change.
[SARAH. Until I speak!]
JAMES: Until you speak—Okay, you wanna play that one—fine with me. Goddamn right! You want to be independent of me, you want to be a person in your own right, you want people not to pity you, but you want them to understand you in the very poetic way you describe in your speech as well as the plain old, boring way *normal* people understand each other, then you learn to read my lips and you learn to use that little mouth of yours for something besides eating and showing me you're better than hearing girls in bed! Come on! Read my lips! What am I saying? Say what I'm saying! What. Am. I. Saying? *(Sarah starts to sign something. HE pins her arms. The rest of this is unsigned)* Shut up! You want to talk to me, then you learn *my* language! Did you get that? Of course you did. You've probably been reading lips perfectly for years; but it's a great control game, isn't it? You can cook, but you can't speak. You can drive and shop and play bridge, but you can't

42

speak. You can even make a speech, but you still can't do it alone. You always have to be dependent on someone, and you always will for the rest of your life until you learn to speak. Now come on! I want you to speak to me. Let me hear it. Speak! Speak! Speak! *(She erupts like a volcano in speech. She doesn't sign.)*

CLOUD NINE   Caryl Churchill

1980s. A park bench in London. MARTIN *(30s) and* VICTORIA *have an up and down but liberated marriage. It lacks tenderness and passion. In a moment abstracted from the ongoing action,* MARTIN *reflects on the freedom* HE *thinks* HE *has given* VICTORIA. *This is to* VICTORIA *who is frozen on-stage.*

MARTIN: So I lost my erection last night not because I'm not prepared to talk, it's just that taking in technical information in a different part of the brain and also I don't like to feel that you do it better to yourself. I have read the *Hite* report. I do know that women have to learn to get their pleasure despite our clumsy attempts at expressing undying devotion and ecstasy, and that what we spent our adolescence thinking was an animal urge we had to suppress is in fact a fine art we have to acquire. I'm not like whatever percentage of American men have become impotent as a direct result of women's liberation, which I am totally in favor of, more I sometimes think than you are yourself. Nor am I one of your villains who sticks it in, bangs away, and falls asleep. My one aim is to give you pleasure. My one aim is to give you rolling orgasms like I do other women. So why the hell don't you have them? My analysis for what it's worth is that despite all my efforts you still feel dominated by me. I in fact think it's very sad that you don't feel able to take that job. It makes me feel very guilty. I don't want you to do it just because I encourage you to do it. But don't you think you'd feel better if you did take the job? You're the one who's talked about freedom. You're the one who's experimenting with bi-sexuality, and I don't stop you, I think women have something to give each other. You seem to need the mutual support. You find me too overwhelming. So follow it through, go away, leave me and Tommy alone for a bit, we can manage perfectly well without you. I'm not putting any pressure on you but I don't think you're being a whole person. God knows I do everything I can to make you stand on your own two feet. Just be yourself. You don't seem to realise how insulting it is to me that you can't get yourself together.

THE COLORED MUSEUM   George C. Wolfe

The present or the recent past. JUNIE ROBINSON *(20s), a combat soldier, comes back to life to tell the story of* HIS *death. Somewhat dimwitted,* JUNIE *has an easy going charm about* HIM. *This is* HIS *only appearance in the play.*

JUNIE: *Pst. Pst.* I know the secret. The secret to your pain. Course I didn't always know. First I had to die, then come back to life, 'fore I had the gift.

Ya see the cappin sent me off up ahead to scout for screamin yella bastards. Course for the life of me I couldn't understand why they'd be screamin seein as how we was tryin to kill them and they us.

But anyway, I'm off lookin, when all of a sudden I find myself caught smack dead in the middle of this explosion. This blindin, burnin, scaldin, explosion. Musta been a booby trap or somethin, cause all around me is fire. Hell I'm on fire. Like a piece of chicken dropped in a skillet of cracklin grease. Why my flesh was justa a peelin off of my bones.

But then I says to myself, "Junie, if yo' flesh is on fire, how come you don't feel no pain." And I didn't. I swear as I'm standin here, I felt nuthin. That's when I sort of put two and two together and realized I didn't feel no whole lot of hurtin cause I done died.

Well, I just picked myself up and walked right on out of that explosion. Hell once you know you dead, why keep on dyin, ya know.

So like I say, I walk right outta that explosion, fully expectin to see white clouds, Jesus and my Mama, only all I saw was more war. Shootin goin on way off in this direction and that direction. And there, standin around, was all the guys. Hubert, J.F., the Cappin. I guess the sound of the explosion must of attracted 'em, and they all starin at me like I'm some kind of ghost.

So I yells to 'em. "Hey there Hubert! Hey there Cappin!" But they just stare. So I tells 'em how I'd died and how I guess it wasn't my time cause here I am. "Fully in the flesh and not a scratch to my bones." And they still just stare. So I took to starin back.

(The expression on JUNIE'S *face slowly turns to horror and disbelief)*

Only what I saw . . . well I can't exactly to this day describe it. But I swear, as sure as they was wearin green and holding guns, they was each wearin a piece of the future on their faces.

Yeah. All the hurt that was gonna get done to them and they was gonna do to folks was right there clear as day.

I saw how J.F., once he got back to Chicago, was gonna get shot dead by this po-lice, and I saw how Hubert was gonna start beatin up on his old lady which I didn't understand, cause all he could do was talk on and on about how much he loved her. Each and every-one of 'em had pain in his future and blood on his path. And God or the devil one spoke to me and said, "Junie, these colored boys ain't gonna be the same after this war. They ain't gonna have no kind of happiness."

Well right then and there it come to me. The secret to their pain.

Late that night, after the medics done checked me over and found me fit for fightin, after everybody done settle down for the night, I sneaked over to where Hubert was sleepin, and with a needle I stole from the medics ... *pst* ... *pst* ... I shot a little air into his veins. The second he died, all the hurtin-to-come just left his face.

Two weeks later I got J.F. and after that Woodrow ... Jimmy Joe ... I even spent all night waitin by the latrine cause I knew the Cappin always made a late night visit and *pst* ... *pst* ... I got him.

(Smiling, quite proud of himself)

That's how come I died and come back to life. Cause just like Jesus went around healin the sick, I'm supposed to go around healin the hurtin all these colored boys wearin from the war.

Pst. Pst. I know the secret. The secret to your pain. The secret to yours, and yours. *Pst. Pst. Pst. Pst.*

DANCING BEARS   Stuart Browne

"F" *steps into the light of a blue special.* HE *is wearing only his jockey shorts.* HE *sings in a high falsetto. What* HE *describes is* HIS *passage from fetus through Cesarian birth and* HIS *mother's death.*

F:
O! FOR THE WINGS!
FOR THE WINGS OF A DOVE!
FAR AWAY, FAR AWAY WOULD I ROAM.
O! FOR THE WINGS!
FOR THE WINGS OF A DOVE ...

... and she is singing happily and sending the song down through her veins and membranes into my belly. I can hear the tune through her water, my eyes not yet opened. Zero gravity. I float. She is moving around a lot. And as her heavy hips sway from side to side, I try to sing along with her as my hair sweeps her soft walls in a slow rhythm, in the dark.

But try as hard as I can, my mouth can make no sound.

So I kick out hard and punch with my tiny fists, trying to applaud her. She stops singing and drops her hands to feel me. She laughs. She throws herself back onto the bed, and I spin a dizzy spin on my Aries Axis.

Sometimes I hear the song in her dreams as I float through the night closed-eyed yet awake. The water would be colder and I would feel what I shall come to know as alone and afraid. So, clenched-fisted, I drum her into waking. She stirs with words on her lips: "Why so early? Why so late?" And we move together across the room to find the lightswitch . . . and I feel the beginnings of a smile. *(Singing)*

O! FOR THE WINGS
FOR THE WINGS OF A DOVE . . .
FAR AWAY . . .
FAR AWAY . . . WOULD I . . .

Now the walls are closing in on me with every heartbeat . . . every breath. And her song begins to get louder . . . but it comes less often. When it does it comes to me through the base of my spine because I am no longer floating free. My head, swollen, blood filled is held firm in her flesh vice. I bite with my toothless gums at the wall and there is a rushing of air above and a doubling up below. The song stops. I am being crushed. I kick and I claw until I feel blood on my fingertips. No song for a moment. Now there it is again. My new bones are bent to breaking, and her lungs, her heart, her liver are pushing for their lives onto the soles of my feet. As she moans above me, I open my mouth. No sound.

O! FOR THE WINGS . . .
FOR THE WINGS OF
A . . . DOVE . . . FAR . . . AWAY—

47

Soon I am buried under new sounds. I feel her gasping as her body tightens around mine. Faster and harder. No singing now. I am about to explode. Through our walls many voices. Now silence. Then the breathing. Silence. Voices. Now the only sounds are small and sharp as the breathing slows to almost no breathing at all. Her song is still elsewhere.

I try to turn my head. Above and to the side I can feel her body parting. I turn. I see the flash of the knife as it comes through her belly and into my cheek. And I am out in the cold. Air!

I look back down at my home. Is she sleeping? I try to cry out . . . no sound . . . no song. I am swinging there, upside down, fire in my ankles. Then I hear the swish and I feel the sting and I pull the first cold air into my new lungs. I scream out for her. She is silent. And I scream and I scream and as my first voice runs around the shining room, I see that same blade, out from the corner of my new eyes, arcing to my center where her voice used to come to me . . .

So now you've heard it. I was knifed in the womb and I've been killing ever since.

DANNY AND THE DEEP BLUE SEA
John Patrick Shanley

The present. A bar in the Bronx. DANNY *(29), "violent, battered, inarticulate and yearning to speak," tells* ROBERTA *that* HE *thinks* HE *killed a guy in a fight last night. The incident gives* DANNY *a chance to release some of* HIS *pent-up rage.*

DANNY: I was at this party. A guy named Skull. Everybody was getting fucked up. Somebody said there was some guys outside. I went out. There were these two guys from another neighborhood out there. I asked 'em what they were doing there. They knew somebody. One of 'em was a big guy. Real drunk. He said they wanted to go, but something about twenty dollars. I told him to give me the twenty dollars, but he didn't have it. I started hitting him. But when I hit him, it never seemed to be hard, you know? I hit him a lot in the chest and face but it didn't seem to do nothing. I had him over a car hood. His friend wanted to take him away. I said okay. They started to go down the block. And they started to fight. So I ran after them. I hit on the little guy a minute, and then I started working on the big guy again. Everybody just watched. I hit him as hard as I could for about ten minutes. It never seemed like enough. Then I looked at his face . . . His teeth were all broken. He fell down. I stomped on his fuckin chest and I heard something break. I grabbed him under the arms and pushed him over a little fence. Into somebody's driveway. Somebody pointed to some guy and said he had the twenty dollars. I kicked him in the nuts. He went right off the ground. Then I left. [. . .] Everybody makes me mad. That's why I don't ever talk to nobody. That's why I'm sittin in this fuckin bar. I don't feel like walkin home. I feel like I'm gonna have to fight everybody in the whole fuckin Bronx to get home. And I'm too tired to fight everybody.

THE DRESSER   Ronald Harwood

January 1942. Backstage of a provincial theatre during the Blitz in wartime England. The events happen before, during and after a climactic performance of KING LEAR. *NORMAN (30s-40s), the dresser who waits hand and foot on the imperious actor/manager,* SIR, *gives these two related monologues. The first comes right after* SIR *has been taken seriously ill.* NORMAN *is talking to the lead actress,* HER LADYSHIP, *about how* HE *got involved with* SIR. *The second is right after* SIR *has died, as* NORMAN *explodes in fear, confusion and frustration over the actor's death to another actress,* MADGE. *In the latter monologue,* NORMAN *quotes the* FOOL's *lines from* KING LEAR.

[HER LADYSHIP: I never imagined it would end like this. I've always thought he was indestructible.]
NORMAN: This'll be the first time we've ever cancelled. I want to go to the hospital—
[HER LADYSHIP: No, Norman—]
NORMAN: I want to sit with him and be with him and try to give him comfort. I can usually make him smile. Perhaps when he sees me—
[HER LADYSHIP: They wouldn't even let me stay.]
(NORMAN fights tears. Pause)

NORMAN: Sixteen years. I wish I could remember the name of the girl who got me into all this. Motherly type she was, small parts, play as cast. I can see her face clearly. I can see her standing there, Platform 2 at Crewe. A Sunday. I was on Platform 4. "Norman," she called. We'd been together in *Outward Bound,* the Number Three tour, helped with wardrobe I did, understudied Scrubby, the steward. That's all aboard a ship, you know. Lovely first act. "We're all dead, aren't we?" And I say, "Yes, Sir, we're all dead. Quite dead." and he says, "How long have you been—

50

you been—oh you know?" "Me, Sir? Oh, I was lost young." And he says, "Where—where are we sailing for?" And I say, "Heaven, Sir. And hell, too. It's the same place, you see." Lovely. Anyway. "Norman!" she called. What was her name? She'd joined Sir, oh, very hoity-toity, I thought, tiaras and blank verse while I was in panto understudying the Ugly Sisters. Both of them. "Are you fixed?" she shouted at the top of her voice. Well. To cut a short story shorter, Sir wanted help in the wardrobe and someone to assist generally, but mainly with the storm in *Lear*. I've told you this before, haven't I? Put me on the timpani, he did. On the first night, after the storm, while he was waiting to go on for 'No, you cannot touch me for coining', he called me over. My knees were jelly. "Were you on the timpani tonight?" "Yes, sir," I said, fearing the worst. "Thank you," he said. "You're an artist." I didn't sleep a wink. Next day he asked if I'd be his dresser. *(Pause)* Madge. You can always tell. She walks as if the band were playing Onward Christian Soldiers.

* * *

(MADGE *takes* SIR's *Lear cloak and covers the* BODY *with it*)
NORMAN: What's to happen to me?
[MADGE: Close the door. Wait outside.]
NORMAN: You're nothing now, ducky. He took away your stripes. And mine. How could he be so bloody careless?
[MADGE: Come away.]
NORMAN: And then where will I go? Where? I'm nowhere out of my element. I don't want to end up running a boarding house in Westcliff-on-Sea. Or Colwyn Bay. What am I going to do?
[MADGE: You can speak well of him.]
NORMAN: Speak well of that old sod? I wouldn't give him a good character, not in a court of law. Ungrateful bastard. Silence, ducky. My lips are sealed.
[MADGE: Get out. I don't want you in here.]

51

NORMAN: Holy, holy, holy, is it? Are we in a shrine? No pissing on the altar—

[MADGE: Stop it.]

NORMAN: He never once took me out for a meal. Never once. Always a back seat, me. Can't even remember him buying me a drink. And just walks out, leaves me, no thought for anyone but himself. What have I been doing here all these years? Why? *(HE turns away from her)* Speak well of him? I know what you'd say, ducky. I know all about you. I've got eyes in my head. We all have our little sorrows. *(MADGE goes but NORMAN does not notice)* I know what you'd say, stiff upper, faithful, loyal. Loving. Well, I have only one thing to say about him and I wouldn't say it in front of you—or Her Ladyship, or anyone. Lips tight shut. I wouldn't give you the pleasure. Or him. Specially not him. If I said what I have to say he'd find a way to take it out on me. No one will ever know. We all have our little sorrows, ducky, you're not the only one. The littler you are, the larger the sorrow. You think *you* loved him? What about me? *(Long silence)* This is not a place for death. I had a friend—*(HE turns suddenly as if aware of someone behind him, but realises HE is alone)* Sir? Sir? *(Silence. HE hugs the exercise book. HE sings—)* "He that has a tiny wit, With hey, ho, the wind and the rain," *(HE falls silent. HE stares into space, Lights fade.)*

52

THE ELEPHANT MAN   Bernard Pomerance

The 1880s. Whitechapel Hospital, London. JOHN MERRICK, *whose grotesque appearance leads to* HIM *being called* THE ELEPHANT MAN, *is under the care and protection of* DR. FREDERICK TREVES *(31).* MERRICK *is the subject of this lecture by* TREVES.

*(*TREVES *lectures.* MERRICK *contorts himself to approximate projected slides of the real Merrick.)*

TREVES: The most striking feature about him was his enormous head. Its circumference was about that of a man's waist. From the brow there projected a huge bony mass like a loaf, while from the back of his head hung a bag of spongy fungous-looking skin, the surface of which was comparable to brown cauliflower. On the top of the skull were a few long lank hairs. The osseous growth on the forehead, at this stage about the size of a tangerine, almost occluded one eye. From the upper jaw there projected another mass of bone. It protruded from the mouth like a pink stump, turning the upper lip inside out, and making the mouth a wide slobbering aperture. The nose was merely a lump of flesh, only recognizable as a nose from its position. The deformities rendered the face utterly incapable of the expression of any emotion whatsoever. The back was horrible because from it hung, as far down as the middle of the thigh, huge sacklike masses of flesh covered by the same loathsome cauliflower stain. The right arm was of enormous size and shapeless. It suggested but was not elephantiasis, and was overgrown also with pendant masses of the same cauliflower-like skin. The right hand was large and clumsy—a fin or paddle rather than a hand. No distinction existed between the palm and back, the thumb was like a radish, the fingers like thick tuberous roots. As a limb it was useless. The other arm was remarkable by contrast. It was not only normal, but was moreover a delicately shaped limb covered with a

53

fine skin and provided with a beautiful hand which any woman might have envied. From the chest hung a bag of the same repulsive flesh. It was like a dewlap suspended from the neck of a lizard. The lower limbs had the characters of the deformed arm. They were unwieldy, dropsical-looking, and grossly misshapen. There arose from the fungous skin growths a very sickening stench which was hard to tolerate. To add a further burden to his trouble, the wretched man when a boy developed hip disease which left him permanently lame, so that he could only walk with a stick. *(To* MERRICK*)* Please. *(*MERRICK *walks.)* He was thus denied all means of escape from his tormentors.

END OF THE WORLD   Arthur Kopit

The present. A suburban house in Connecticut. MICHAEL TRENT *(40s), a playwright who goes about* HIS *business like a private detective, has been commissioned to write a play about nuclear doom by the mysterious and sinister* PHILIP STONE. *At the end of the play,* TRENT *realizes that* HE *cannot complete the doom play. In a moment of recognition,* TRENT *suddenly connects* STONE *with a frightening incident years earlier.*

TRENT: Now I know where we met! . . . It was at *our* place, our apartment! We were living in the city then, and some friends came by to see our child, he'd just been born; obviously, one of them brought Stone—who? doesn't matter, Stone was there, I can see him, in a corner, *listening,* as I . . . tell. *(Pause)* But *evil?* *(Long pause)* Our son had just been born. We'd brought him home. He was what, five days old, I guess. *(Pause)* And then one day my wife went out . . . And I was left alone with him. And I was very excited. Because it was the first time I was alone with him. And I picked him up, this tiny thing, and started walking around the living room. We lived on a high floor, overlooking the river, the Hudson.

Light was streaming in; it was a lovely, lilting autumn day, cool, beautiful. And I looked down at this tiny creature, this tiny thing, and I realized . . . *(Pause)* I realized I had never had anyone completely in my power before! . . . And I'd never known what that *meant!* Never felt anything remotely like that before! And I saw I was standing near a window. And it was open. It was but a few feet away. And I thought: I could . . . *drop him out!* And I went *toward* the window, because I couldn't believe this thought had come into my head—*where had it come from?* Not one part of me felt anything for this boy but love, not one part! My wife and I had planned, we were both in love, there was no anger, no resentment, nothing dark in me toward him at all, no one could ever have been more in love with his child than I, as much yes, but not more, not more, and I was thinking: I can throw him out of here! . . . and then he will be falling ten, twelve, fifteen, twenty stories down, and as he's falling, I will be *unable to get him back!* . . . And I felt a *thrill!* I FELT A THRILL! IT WAS THERE! . . . And, of course, I resisted this. It wasn't hard to do, resisting wasn't hard . . . BUT I DIDN'T STAY BY THE WINDOW! . . . AND I CLOSED IT! I resisted by moving away, back into the room . . . And I sat down with him. *(Pause)* Well, there's not a chance I would have done it, not a chance! *(Pause)* But I couldn't *take* a chance, it was very, very . . . seductive. *(Pause. HE looks at STONE. The lights come back a bit. STONE is sipping his tea, eyes on TRENT)* If doom comes . . . it will come in *that* way.

*It is 1957. The porch and yard of a house in urban Pittsburgh.
TROY MAXSON (53) is the proud patriarch of a black family. HE
is a big man who was once a talented baseball player. HE now
works as a city trash collector and has learned to fight for HIS little
victories. In the first monologue, HE reacts sternly when HIS son,
CORY, asks why TROY has never liked HIM. In the second
monologue, TROY has just heard from HIS wife, ROSE, that HIS
mistress, ALBERTA, died in childbirth. HE reacts angrily and
challenges DEATH.*

[CORY: How come you ain't never liked me?]

TROY: Liked you? Who the hell say I got to like you? What law
is there say I got to like you? Wanna stand up in my face and ask a
damn fool-ass question like that. Talking about liking somebody.
Come here, boy, when I talk to you

*(CORY comes over to where TROY is working. HE stands
slouched over and TROY shoves HIM on HIS shoulder)*

Straighten up, goddammit! I asked you a question. What law is
there say I got to like you?

[CORY: None.]

TROY: Well, all right then! Don't you eat every day?

(Pause)

Answer me when I talk to you! Don't you eat every day?

[CORY: Yeah.]

TROY: Nigger, as long as you in my house you put that sir on the
end of it when you talk to me!

[CORY: Yes . . . sir.]

TROY: You eat every day. Got a roof over your head. Got
clothes on your back.

[CORY: Yessir.]

TROY: Why you think that is?

[CORY: 'Cause of you.]

TROY: Aw, hell I know it's 'cause of me . . . but why do you think that is?

[CORY: *(Hesitant)* 'Cause you like me.]

TROY: Like you? I go out of here every morning, bust my butt, putting up with them crackers every day . . . 'cause I like you? You about the biggest fool I ever saw.

(Pause)

It's my job. It's my responsibility! You understand that? A man got to take care of his family. You live in my house, sleep you behind on my bedclothes, fill you belly up with my food . . . 'cause you my son. You my flesh and blood. Not 'cause I like you! 'Cause I owe a responsibility to you! 'Cause it's my duty to take care of you. Let's get this straight right here—before it go along any further—I ain't got to like you. Mr. Rand don't give me my money come payday 'cause he likes me. He gives me 'cause he owe me. I done give you everything I had to give you. I gave you your life! Me and your mama worked that out between us. And liking your black ass wasn't part of the bargain. Don't you try and go through life worrying about if somebody like you or not. You best be making sure they doing right by you. You understand what I'm saying, boy?

[CORY: Yessir.]

TROY: Then get the hell out of my face, and get on down to that A & P.

* * *

[ROSE: Troy, you ain't got to talk like that.]

TROY: That's the first thing that jumped out your mouth. "Who's gonna bury her?" Like I'm fixing to take on that task for myself.

[ROSE: I am your wife. Don't push me away.]

TROY: I ain't pushing nobody away. Just give me some space. That's all. Just give me some room to breathe.

(ROSE exits into the house. TROY walks about the yard)

TROY: *(With a quiet rage that threatens to consume him)* All right, Mr. Death. See now . . . I'm gonna tell you what I'm gonna do. I'm gonna take and build me a fence around this yard. See? I'm gonna build me a fence around what belongs to me. And then I want you to stay on the other side. See? You stay over there until you're ready for me. Then you come on. Bring your army. Bring your sickle. Bring your wrestling clothes. I ain't gonna fall down on my vigilance this time. You ain't gonna sneak up on me no more. When you ready for me, when the top of your list say Troy Maxson, that's when you come around here. You come up and knock on the front door and ask for me. Then we gonna find out what manner of man you are. Ain't nobody else got nothing to do with this. This is between you and me. Man to man. You stay on the other side of that fence until you ready for me. Then you come up and knock on the front door. Anytime you want. I'll be ready for you.

(The lights go down to black.)

FIVE OF US   Len Jenkin

The present. A New York City apartment. MARK (30s) is a professional writer who makes a living churning out porno novels. HE has several in progress at once on three different typewriters. But HE keeps HIS "serious" novel hidden away in a drawer as if it were a piece of forbidden pornography. HE talks about this novel to two women friends, CRYSTAL and LEE, who badger HIM into telling them what it's about. But MARK has trouble articulating just what it is about.

MARK: *(Closing the manuscript drawer)* Not to worry. Once this novel is out I get into the true art form of the eighties—retailing. Major motion pictures will be offered to me—by telephone. I'll speak at college graduations, tell them about the virtues of hard work. Then—late in life—politics.[. . .] My book is about a man who is trying to write a book. The book *he's* trying to write is about this man, see, who's trying to write a book. That man's book is about[. . .]O.K. The book's just about some people hanging around on the planet, trying to find out how to live and be happy—plus there's major digressions on clocks, dancing, mirrors and death.[. . .] All right. I guess I'm just trying to tell people what I've seen and dreamed—kind of word window in the skull. You know Peter Lorre? Great German actor, came to Hollywood and became a hack with an accent in a bunch of sentimental thrillers. I saw him once on the Ed Sullivan show when I was seven. I remember Ed was introducing him and I knew he didn't sing or dance or tell jokes. I couldn't imagine what he was gonna do. Peter Lorre walked out there, sat on a stool, and did this monologue of a man with a glass head. Anyone can see inside, and his thoughts are there, in pictures, like dreams. Embarrassing. So, he wears a hat. Always. He's an artist—sensitive, unappreciated, broke. He hates the vulgar, pedestrian people around him. One day the wind blows off his hat. It's gone. He's gotta get home. He gets on a bus, and a real prim old lady is looking at him funny. He's thinking how he'd like to bury a hatchet in her face and watch her bloody forehead split in two—and the old lady screams. She can see him, murdering her in his head. She's freaking out, and everyone on the bus rises up, staring into his head, ready to kill the little monster. He's terrified. He runs. He makes it home to his little room. He sits there at the mirror, staring into the red fever swirling in his skull.

Ten years later *I'm* riding a bus and I finally get it. He didn't have a glass head. He believed that other people knew his thoughts, and this forced him to confront his own bloody and useless mind *at every moment*. So, he cracked, or maybe he faced it all and came through. I don't know. I do know he had a head just like yours or mine. Except Peter Lorre's face was on it . . . Why did I tell that story?

FOB   David Henry Hwang

The present. California. A stage with a blackboard. DALE *(20s),
an American-born Chinese dressed as a preppie, delivers this Pro-
logue to the audience.* HE *lectures like a university professor about
the characteristics of the* FOB, *using the blackboard to illustrate* HIS
points.

DALE: F-O-B. Fresh Off the Boat. FOB. What words can you
think of that characterize the FOB? Clumsy, ugly, greasy FOB.
Loud, stupid, four-eyed FOB. Big feet. Horny. Like Lenny in *Of
Mice and Men*. Very good. A literary reference. High water pants.
Floods, to be exact. Someone you wouldn't want your sister to
marry. If you are a sister, someone you wouldn't want to marry.
That assumes we're talking about boy FOBs, of course. But girl
FOBs aren't really as . . . FOBish. Boy FOBs are the worst, the
. . . pits. They are the sworn enemies of all ABC—Oh, that's
"American-Born Chinese"—Of all ABC girls. Before an ABC girl
will be seen on Friday night with a boy FOB in Westwood, she
would rather burn off her face. *(HE flips around the board. On the
other side is written: "1. Where to find FOBs 2. How to spot a
FOB")* FOBs can be found in great numbers almost anyplace you
happen to be, but there are some locations where they cluster in particularly large swarms. Community colleges, Chinese-club discos,
Asian sororities, Asian fraternities, Oriental churches, shopping
malls, and, of course, Bee Gee concerts. How can you spot a
FOB? Look out! If you can't answer that, you might be one. *(HE
flips back the board, reviews)* F-O-B. Fresh Off the Boat. FOB.
Clumsy, ugly, greasy FOB. Loud, stupid, four-eyed FOB. Big
feet. Horny. Like Lenny in *Of Mice and Men*. Floods. Like
Lenny in *Of Mice and Men*. F-O-B. Fresh Off the Boat. FOB.

FOOL FOR LOVE   Sam Shepard

*The present. Stark, low-rent motel room on the edge of the Mojave
Desert, California.* THE OLD MAN *(60s-70s) sits in a rocker in
slight profile to the audience. A bottle of whiskey sits on the floor
beside* HIM. HE *has a scraggly, red beard, wears an old, stained,
"open road" Stetson hat and mismatched, beat-up, Western clothes.
HE exists only in the mind of* MAY *and* EDDIE. *In the first monologue,* THE OLD MAN *tells a story to* MAY *while she is crawling
around the walls of the motel room. It is a comforting image of
childhood. In the second monologue,* EDDIE *tells a story to* MAR-
TIN *about* THE OLD MAN's *philandering and* HIS *first sight of*
MAY.

THE OLD MAN: Ya' know, one thing I'll never forget. I'll
never forget this as long as I live—and I don't even know why I
remember it exactly. We were drivin' through southern Utah once,
I think it was. Me, you and your mother—in that old Plymouth we
had. You remember that Plymouth? Had a white plastic hood ornament on it. Replica of the *Mayflower* I think it was. Some kind
a' ship. Anyway, we'd been drivin' all night and you were sound
asleep in the front. And all of a sudden you woke up crying. Just
bustin' a gut over somethin'. I don't know what it was. Nightmare
or somethin'. Woke your mom right up and she climbed over the
seat in back there with you to try to get you settled down. But you
wouldn't shut up for hell or high water. Just kept wailing away.
So I stopped the Plymouth by the side of the road. Middle a'
nowhere. I can't even remember where it was exactly. Pitch black.
I picked you up outa' the back seat there and carried you into this
field. Thought the cold air might quiet you down a little bit. But
you just kept on howling away. Then, all of a sudden, I saw
somethin' move out there. Somethin' bigger than both of us put together. And it started to move toward us kinda' slow.

(MAY begins to crawl slowly on her hands and knees from

down-right corner toward bed. When she reaches bed, she grabs
pillow and embraces it, still on her knees. She rocks back and forth
embracing pillow as THE OLD MAN *continues)*

And then it started to get joined up by some other things just like it. Same shape and everything. It was so black out there I could hardly make out my own hand. But these things started to kinda' move in on us from all directions in a big circle. And I stopped dead still and turned back to the car to see if your mother was all right. But I couldn't see the car anymore. So I called out to her. I called her name loud and clear. And she answered me back from outa' the darkness. She yelled back to me. And just then these things started to "moo." They all started "mooing" away.

(HE makes the sound of a cow)

And it turns out, there we were, standin' smack in the middle of a goddamn herd of cattle. Well, you never heard a baby pipe down so fast in your life. You never made a peep after that. The whole rest of the trip.

* * *

EDDIE: Well, see—*(Pause,* HE *stares at* THE OLD MAN*)*—our daddy fell in love twice. That's basically how it happened. Once with my mother and once with her mother.[. . .] He had two separate lives.[. . .] Two completely separate lives. He'd live with me and my mother for a while and then he'd disappear and go live with her and her mother for a while.[. . .] He'd disappear for months at a time and she never once asked him where he went. She was always glad to see him when he came back. The two of us used to go running out of the house to meet him as soon as we saw the Studebaker coming across the field.[. . .] This went on for years. He kept disappearing and reappearing. For years that went on. Then, suddenly, one day it stopped. He stayed home for a while. Just stayed in the house. Never went outside. Just sat in his chair. Staring. Then he started going on these long walks. He'd

62

walk all day. Then he'd walk all night. He'd walk out across the fields. In the dark. I used to watch him from my bedroom window. He'd disappear in the dark with his overcoat on.[. . .] Just walking. (EDDIE *gets* MARTIN *to his feet and takes him on a walk around the entire stage as he tells the story.* MARTIN *is reluctant but* EDDIE *keeps pulling him along*)

EDDIE: But one night I asked him if I could go with him. And he took me. We walked straight out across the fields together. In the dark. And I remember it was just plowed and our feet sank down in the powder and the dirt came up over the tops of my shoes and weighed me down. I wanted to stop and empty my shoes out but he wouldn't stop. He kept walking straight ahead and I was afraid of losing him in the dark so I just kept up as best I could. And we were completely silent the whole time. Never said a word to each other. We could barely see a foot in front of us, it was so dark. And these white owls keep swooping down out of nowhere, hunting for jackrabbits. Diving right past our heads, then disappearing. And we just kept walking silent like that for miles until we got to town. I could see the drive-in movie way off in the distance. That was the first thing I saw. Just square patches of color shifting. Then vague faces began to appear. And, as we got closer, I could recognize one of the faces. It was Spencer Tracy. Spencer Tracy moving his mouth. Speaking without words. Speaking to a woman in a red dress. Then we stopped at a liquor store and he made me wait outside in the parking lot while he bought a bottle. And there were all these Mexican migrant workers standing around a pickup truck with red mud all over the tires. They were drinking beer and laughing and I remember being jealous of them and I didn't know why. And I remember seeing the old man through the glass door of the liquor store as he paid for the bottle. And I remember feeling sorry for him and I didn't know why. Then he came outside with the bottle wrapped in a brown paper sack and as soon as he came out, all the Mexican men stopped laughing. They just stared at us as we walked away.[. . .] And we walked right through town. Past the donut shop, past the miniature golf course, past the Chevron station. And he opened the bottle up and offered it to me. Before he even took a drink, he offered it to me first. And I took it and drank it and handed it back to him. And we just kept passing it back and forth like that as we walked until we drank the whole thing dry. And we never said a word the whole time. Then, finally, we reached this little white house with a red awning, on the far side of town. I'll never forget the red awning because it flapped in the night breeze and the porch light made it glow. It was a hot, desert breeze and the air smelled like new-cut alfalfa. We walked right up to the front porch and he rang the bell and I remember getting real nervous because I wasn't expecting to visit anybody. I thought we were just out for a walk. And this this woman comes to the door. This real pretty woman with red hair. And she throws herself into his arms. And he starts crying. He just breaks down right there in front of me. And she's kissing him all over the face and holding him real tight and he's just crying like a baby. And then through the doorway, behind them both, I see this girl.

(The bathroom door very slowly and silently swings open revealing MAY, *standing in the doorframe backlit with yellow light in her red dress. She just watches* EDDIE *as* HE *keeps telling story.* HE *and* MARTIN *are unaware of her presence)*

EDDIE: She just appears. She's just standing there, staring at me and I'm staring back at her and we can't take our eyes off each other. It was like we knew each other from somewhere but we couldn't place where. But the second we saw each other, that very second, we knew we'd never stop being in love.

FUNHOUSE   Eric Bogosian

FUNHOUSE *is a series of monologue sketches written by ERIC*
BOGOSIAN and performed by HIM *as a full evening. The mono-*
logues take as their characters different urban types whose yearnings
and language reveal a darker side of the 1980s. There are no spe-
cific indications for the performance of these selfcontained pieces.
But each requires an intense delivery.

In the Dark
A voice begins in darkness. Slowly lights come up on a man at a
table speaking into a microphone.

I wait for dark, the black comes for me. Some people are afraid
when the sun goes down. But for me, for me it's good in the deep
dark. Warm and dark and close. Some people are afraid of small
places, tight spots, restrictive. Not me. I'm in the right place, the
good dark place. Like a baby in its womb, like a rat in its
hole . . . I'm OK.

Ever see the black skid marks out on the highway? Ever wonder
what happened? I don't. I think about the tires, the rubber
. . . the black rubber. Burning. Melting. Pouring down in ropes,
in sheets, in long black ribbons all around me. Twisting all around
me. Around and around. Black and tight, close and dark. Holding
me. Hiding me in the darkness . . .

Don't you love the smell of black rubber? The way it feels
against the skin? Maybe not, it's an acquired taste. Some people
never get used to it.

You can work your way up: black leather, then black spandex,
then black rubber. Tight. Black. Rubber. Up against you. Press-
ing. Keeping. Holding. Resilient but firm. Every muscle, every
inch is encased in pure black . . .

The arms, the legs, the chest, the groin, the head. All smooth, all
black . . . completely hidden. In my black cocoon I'm where no

one can find me, no one can hurt me, no one can touch me. I'm safe in the dark, I'm happy in my hiding place.

I don't have to think, I don't have to feel . . . and the best part is . . . I don't have to see . . .

* * *

Sitcom

A man picks up the phone at a table, answering in a shrill, fast-talking voice.

Arnie! Arnie! Yeah, yeah, listen. Sid! You got two minutes? Yeah, yeah, listen, I got a great idea for a sitcom . . . sitcom, Arnie, sitcom! Situation comedy, what are you doing up there in your office, take the straw outa ya nose for two minutes and listen to me for a second. Arnie! Arnie! Concentrate! Follow me.

Scenario: New York City! Apartment building in New York. Black guy lives in the apartment. Nice black guy, middle-class black guy, button-down-sweater type of guy, smokes a pipe. Yeah, yeah . . . harmless black guy. Benson! Benson! We got Benson in this apartment . . . Across the hall from him, paraplegic kid in a wheelchair . . . Huh? You don't need a real one, you just get any cute kid and stick him in a wheelchair. What? Fuck the unions! The kid's in a wheelchair here, black guy across the hall. They got a real nice relationship here. Big brother, interracial kind of thing. Yeah. Mushy liberal stuff . . . a show with meaning . . . Yeah, a show with relevance to the social problems of today . . . yeah, yeah, *Mary Tyler Moore, Hill Street, M*A*S*H, Cosby, The Waltons!*

Wait, wait, more! Top floor of the building we got a whorehouse! Hookers going up and down stairs all time of night and day. Falling over the kid with the wheelchair, sticking lollipops in his mouth, patting his head. Cute stuff like that, sweet stuff, light humor, family humor . . .

66

Ground floor of the apartment building: gay health club! Homos working out with weights, building up the pectoral muscles ... See what I'm saying? We got the beefcake down here doing sit-ups while the cheesecake's up here doing push-ups! Something for everybody! Wait, wait, one more apartment, teen-age kid living with his mother, OK, this is the humor of the show. Kid wants to kill everybody in New York City! One week he makes an atom bomb in his bedroom, next week he puts LSD in the city water supply, then he derails a subway car, who knows? Crazy stuff, funny stuff, hilarious stuff! We'll call the show *Upstairs, Downstairs* ... Huh? Who's PBS? Fuck PBS! ... Those are little people. They don't count. We'll buy the title off of them ... Arnie, what are you busting my balls about this thing for? Yeah? That was two years ago! Yeah, I know what's good for me. What's good for me is what's good for you! Arnie, we'll have lunch next week and discuss the project, OK? Huh? Look Arnie, I got a call on the other line, I got to get off ... Arnie, I'm getting off ... I'm getting off, Arnie! Arnie ... Arnie ... Arnie ... Good-bye! *(Hangs up.)*

GHOST ON FIRE   Michael Weller

The present. New York City and Maine. DAN (30s) is a teacher and screenwriter. HIS monologue opens the play. ADEN (30s) is DAN's friend and wants to be everyone's friend. Both monologues are to the audience.

DAN: My name is Dan Rittman. I'm a teacher here in New York. Picture this: One morning we wake up to absolute devastation; buildings down, power out, crops dead on the stem, The Apocalypse, whatever. Overnight, we've been reduced to a savage world of kill or be killed, eat or be eaten ... no diversions, no escape to the gym or the movies; no more fancy problems. Suddenly it's *right out there*, bold and simple and deadly. *(Beat)* I have dreams about such a world, vivid dreams. I see my friends for the first time as they truly are; some cunning, some brave, some loyal and strong, others weak and treacherous, but always strikingly different from the way they appear in everyday waking life. And here's what's weird. Sometimes I stop and catch myself longing, desperately longing for such a world, like a great welcome burning away of all the lies and evasions. It's terrifying. I mean, why should I harbor such a deep desire to see the only world I know utterly annihilated? I'm an ordinary person, like you, alive in this most pleasant of centuries, possibly the last, and like you I want nothing more than to get through each day without hassles, doing as little harm as possible, minding my own business. *(Smiles)* I have what I consider to be a highly civilized attitude towards life.

* * *

ADEN: I think I can honestly say I've never met anyone who I didn't find, somehow, absolutely fascinating. In fact, I can't conceive of such a thing as an uninteresting person. Even . . . well, even an insurance salesman from, say, LaPort, Indiana could come up to me and say "Hello there, my name is Bill Smithers and I'm the most boring person in the world," and I just know I'd be thinking, "How fascinating! I wonder what makes him feel he's so boring? I wonder why he chose to tell *me?*" Because I'm sure, at certain moments, perhaps when he's not monitoring his brain too carefully, this man must have the most incredibly unexpected thoughts, even perhaps a little *wild!* He might, for example, picture himself riding naked on back of a very large giraffe and waving to a crowd of frenzied disciples clad in a certain kind of peculiar silver uniform. Or, perhaps he sees himself alone on a remote tropical island with an incredibly beautiful woman. Or an incredibly ugly one. Or perhaps the only person in the world who has such thoughts is *me.* But I just somehow doubt that very much. Now don't misunderstand.

I'm not saying there aren't people who I find just totally obnoxious ... and overbearing ... and rude and even just completely *repellent*. But that doesn't mean they aren't somehow fascinating in their own overbearing and repellent way. I'm sorry, but that's simply how I see things. You may disagree entirely. In fact I hope you do. Because, really, when you think about it, if everyone saw things exactly as I do, well, the world wouldn't be nearly as interesting a place as it is. And that's really all I have to say.

GLENGARRY GLEN ROSS   David Mamet

The present. A seedy Chinese restaurant in Chicago. RICHARD ROMA *(30s-40s), a badgering real estate salesman, is seated in a booth alone.* HE *begins talking across the room to* JAMES LINGK, *whom* HE *doesn't know at all. After a long opening gambit at "heart to heart" conversation,* ROMA *begins zeroing in on* LINGK *for a sales pitch before the blackout.*

ROMA: . . . all train compartments smell vaguely of shit. It gets so you don't mind it. That's the worst thing that I can confess. You know how long it took me to get there? A long time. When you *die* you're going to regret the things you don't do. You think you're *queer* . . . ? I'm going to tell you something: we're *all* queer. You think that you're a *thief?* So *what?* You get befuddled by a middle-class morality . . . ? Get *shut* of it. Shut it out. You cheated on your wife . . . ? You *did* it, *live* with it. *(Pause)* You fuck little girls, so *be* it. There's an absolute morality? May *be.* And *then* what? If you *think* there is, then *be* that thing. Bad people go to hell? I don't *think* so. If you think that, act that way. A hell exists on earth? Yes. I won't live in it. That's *me.* You ever take a dump made you feel you'd just slept for twelve hours . . . ?
[LINGK: Did I . . . ?]
ROMA: Yes.

[LINGK: I don't know.]

ROMA: Or a *piss* ...? A great meal fades in reflection. Everything else gains. You know why? 'Cause it's only food. This shit we eat, it keeps us going. But it's only food. The great fucks that you may have had. What do you remember about them?

[LINGK: What do I ...?]

ROMA: Yes.

[LINGK: Mmmm ...]

ROMA: I don't know. For *me,* I'm saying, what it is, it's probably not the orgasm. Some broads, forearms on your neck, something her *eyes* did. There was a *sound* she made ... or, me, lying, in the, I'll tell you: me lying in bed; the next day she brought me café au lait. She gives me a cigarette, my balls feel like concrete. Eh? What I'm saying, what is our life? *(Pause)* It's looking forward or it's looking back. And that's our life. that's *it.* Where is the *moment? (Pause)* And what is it that we're afraid of? Loss. What else? *(Pause)* The *bank* closes. We get *sick,* my wife died on a plane, the stock market collapsed ... the house burnt down ... what of these happen ...? None of 'em. We worry anyway. What does this mean? I'm not *secure.* How can I be secure? *(Pause)* Through amassing wealth beyond all measure? No. And what's beyond all measure? That's sickness. That's a trap. There is no measure. Only greed. How can we act? The right way, we would say, to deal with this: "There is a one-in-a-million chance that so and so will happen ... *Fuck* it, it won't happen to *me* ... " No. We know that's not the right way I think. *(Pause)* We say the *correct* way to deal with this is "There is a one-in-so-and-so chance this will happen ... God *protect* me. I am powerless, let it not happen to me ... " But no to *that.* I say. There's something else. What is it? "If it happens, AS IT MAY for that is not within our powers, I will *deal* with it, just as I do *today* with what draws my concern today." I say *this* is how we must act. I do those things which seem correct to me *today.* I trust

myself. And if security concerns me, I do that which *today* I think
will make me secure. And every day I *do* that, when that day
arrives that I need a reserve, (a) odds are that I have it, and (b) the
true reserve that I have is the strength that I have of *acting each day*
without fear. *(Pause)* According to the dictates of my mind.
(Pause) Stocks, bonds, objects of art, real estate. Now: what are
they? *(Pause)* An opportunity. To what? To make money? Perhaps. To *lose* money? Perhaps. To "indulge" and to "learn" about
ourselves? Perhaps. *So fucking what?* What *isn't?* They're an
opportunity. That's all. They're an *event*. A guy comes up to you,
you make a call, you send in a brochure, it doesn't matter, "There're
these *properties* I'd like for you to see." What does it mean? What
you *want* it to mean. *(Pause)* Money? *(Pause)* If that's what it sig-
nifies to you. Security? *(Pause)* Comfort? *(Pause)* All it is is
THINGS THAT HAPPEN TO YOU. *(Pause)* That's all it is. How
are they different? *(Pause)* Some poor newly married guy gets run
down by a cab. Some *busboy* wins the lottery. *(Pause)* All it is,
it's a carnival. What's special . . . what *draws* us? *(Pause)*
We're all different. *(Pause)* We're not the same. *(Pause)* We are
not the same. *(Pause)* Hmmm. *(Pause. Sighs)* It's been a long
day. *(Pause)* What are you drinking?
[LINGK: Gimlet]
ROMA: Well, let's have a couple more. My name is Richard
Roma, what's yours?
[LINGK: Lingk. James Lingk.]
ROMA: James. I'm glad to meet you. *(They shake hands)* I'm
glad to meet you, James. *(Pause)* I want to show you something.
(Pause) It might mean *nothing* to you . . . and it might not. I
don't know. I don't know anymore. *(Pause. He takes out a small
map and spreads it on a table)* What is that? Florida. Glengarry
Highlands. Florida. "Florida. *Bullshit.*" And maybe that's true;
and that's what *I* said: but look *here:* what is this? This is a piece
of land. Listen to what I'm going to tell you now:

71

HERRINGBONE   Tom Cone

1929. The start of the Depression. The swimming pool of a motel court in Hollywood, California. GEORGE HERRINGBONE, *the narrator of the play, is played by an actor who assumes all the other roles:* GEORGE *(an eight-year-old child prodigy)*, LOU *(a.k.a. "The Frog," a thirty-five-year-old midget who inhabits* GEORGE's *body and acts as his "manager")*, LOUISE *(GEORGE's stage mother)*, *and* ARTHUR *(GEORGE's passive but avaricious father). The actor must make quick transformations between parts, finding different voices and habits for each role. The adults have brought* GEORGE *to Hollywood to get* HIM *in the movies and make themselves some money. A fight breaks out and* GEORGE *begins to suffer.*

HERRINGBONE: This is the heat of Hollywood. A kidney shaped pool outside a tourist court off The Strip. I was in an inner tube. Kickin' and splashin' away!

GEORGE: *(Doing so)* Red Rover, Red Rover, Let George come over!

LOU: For Christsakes, George!

GEORGE: Don't ya love it, Mr. Lou?

HERRINGBONE: And there was Daddy, dog paddlin' his way over to me with a grin that was needin' a favor.

ARTHUR: *(Water up to his mouth)* Slow down, there, George.

HERRINGBONE: *(Stepping out of this pantomime, referring back to the area where* HE *just created it, and directly asking the audience)* Do I look like I'm swimmin'? Not an easy thing to do, ya know. *(*HE *steps back in)*

ARTHUR: *(Dog-paddling in place)* I've been thinkin' how well we've been doing over the past six weeks and I was wonderin' if we should prepare for the future.

LOU: *(In the inner tube)* You want to continue?

ARTHUR: Well, I don't see why not.

LOU: Excellent.

ARTHUR: I don't want to get caught short-changed again and I wondered if you'd do a favor for your Mamma and I, and sign a will?

LOU: *(Taken aback)* A will? Jesus Christ. *(Starts to go under water)* Help! Help!

LOUISE: *(Her propriety assaulted, SHE stops)* Mr. Lou, now that we've reached Hollywood, I figure that it's time for you to go. According to our agreement? The end of the six weeks? The end of our arrangement?

LOU: Go?

LOUISE: Like you said.

LOU: Well, I don't know about that, Louise.

LOUISE: *(Grabbing him)* Well, I do!

GEORGE: Mother?

LOUISE: Quiet, George. *(To LOU)* You promised!

LOU: *(Shouting so ARTHUR can hear)* Arthur said we could continue!

LOUISE: *(Shaking him)* I'm telling you it's over!

GEORGE: You're squeezing my arm, Mother.

LOUISE: You've got to leave now!

GEORGE: You're hurtin' me, Mother.

LOUISE: I won't take no for an answer!

GEORGE : Mother! Please! *(LOUISE slaps him; is shocked with herself. Long transition as HERRINGBONE steps away from the scene, regards it, leaves it behind emotionally.)*

HUNTING COCKROACHES   Janusz Glowacki

The present. New York. A squalid, shabby apartment during the night. JAN (30s-40s), a Polish émigré writer, sits in a chair studying a map of America. Nearby is a can of roach spray. HIS wife, ANKA, is asleep in bed. HE speaks to the audience.

JAN: What a strange country. I was born in a town that was Polish once, then it was Czech, then it was Austrian, then it was Russian, then it was German, and now it's Communist. When Stalin died, during a memorial ceremony at our school the principal informed us that the leaders of the Polish People's Republic had decided to honor the memory of the best friend Polish children ever had by renaming our school Stalinowka and the town to Stalinowo. So I suggested our principal also be renamed to Joseph Stalin. The colonel in the Secret Police who interrogated me really liked the idea of renaming our principal to Stalin. I was lucky. He not only saved me from prison but he showed a lot of interest in my career, until he was transferred to Rome as an expert on religious affairs. *(HE outlines a map with his finger)* Here's France, and Austria, and Germany, the Soviet Union, Poland. The boundary lines between all the countries twist, and turn, and twitch like worms in a can. Messy. *(Points to American map)* That's what you call a neat job. Look here. . *(Points to states on the map)*, Montana, Wyoming, North Dakota, South Dakota, Missouri *(HE pronounces it "misery")* . . . This country was laid out by someone who had technical training. Buildings *(Traces rectangles in the air)*, streets *(Traces lines)*, everything, even people are well made. That's what you'd call a good piece of work. Only the cockroaches seem not to have come out quite right . . . yet.

HURLYBURLY   David Rabe

*The time is "a little while ago." The living room of a small house in
the Hollywood Hills owned by roommates* EDDIE *and* MICKEY.
*Both work in the "business." Different friends drift in and out of
the house during the action. Here are three different monologues by
the men. The first is by* MICKEY *(30s), an aloof character who
enjoys watching and commenting on the conversations and anxieties
of others. The second is by the out-of-work, out-of-marriage actor
friend,* PHIL *(30s-40s), whose anxiety reaches the breaking-point
when* HE *finds out* HIS *estranged wife is pregnant. The third is
spoken by* EDDIE *(30s), the central character in the play and the one
to whom everyone else confides. Yet* EDDIE *is troubled, drunk and
depressed by just about everything* HE *hears and reads.*

MICKEY: You know what I'm going to do? I'm going to venture
a thought that I might regret down the road. And anticipating that
regret makes me, you know, hesitate. In the second of hesitation, I
get a good look at the real feeling that it is, this regret—a kind of inner blackmail that shows me even further down the road where I
would end up having to live with myself as a smaller person, a man
less generous to his friends than I would care to be. *(Slowly, carefully,* HE *descends the stairs)* So, you know, we'll have to put this
through a multiprocessing here, but I was outside, I mean, for a
while; and what I heard in here was—I mean, it really was passion.
Sure, it was a squabble, and anybody could have heard that, but
what I heard was more. We all know—everybody knows I'm basically on a goof right now. I'm going back to my wife and kids
sooner or later—I don't hide that fact from anybody. And what I
really think is that fact was crucial to the development of this whole
thing because it made me WHAT? Safe. A viable diversion from
what might have actually been a genuine, meaningful, and to that
same extent and maybe even more so—threatening—connection
between you two. I'm not going to pretend I wasn't up for it,

too—but I was never anything but above board. You know—a couple jokes, nice dinner, that's my style. Good wine, we gotta spend the night—and I don't mean to be crass—because the point is maybe we have been made fools of here by our own sophistication, and what am I protecting by not saying something about it, my vanity? Ego? Who needs it? So, I'm out in the yard and I'm thinking, "Here is this terrific guy, this dynamic lady, and they are obviously, definitely hooked up on some powerful, idiosyncratic channel, so what am I doing in the middle?" Am I totally off base here, Eddie, or what?

* * *

PHIL: Eddie, for god sake, don't terrify me that you have paid no attention! If I was thoughtless would I be here? I feel like I have pushed thought to the brink where it is just noise and of no more use than a headful of car horns, because the bottom line here that I'm getting at is just this—I got to go back to her. I got to go back to Susie, and if it means havin'a kid, I got to do it. I mean, I have hit a point where I am going round the bend several times a day now, and so far I been on the other side to meet me, but one of these days it might be one time too many, and who knows who might be there waitin'? If not me, who? I'm a person, Eddie, and I have realized it, who needs like a big-dot-thing, you know—this big-dot-thing around which I can just hang and blab my thoughts and more or less formulate everything as I go, myself included. I mean, I used to spend my days in my car; I didn't know what the fuck I was doin' but it kept me out of trouble until nothin' but blind luck led me to I-am-married, and I could go home. She was my big-dot-thing. Now I'm startin' in my car again. I'm spendin' days on the freeways and rain or no rain I like the wipers clickin', and all around me the other cars got people in 'em the way I see them when they are in cars. These heads, these faces. These boxes of steel with glass and faces inside. I been the last three days without seeing another form

76

of human being in his entirety except gas station attendants. The family men in the day with their regular food and regular hours in their eyes. And then in the night, these moonlighters; they could be anything. In the wee hours of the morning, it's derelicts, and these weird spooky kids like they have recently arrived from outer space, but not to stay. The cloverleafs, they got a thing in them, it spins me off. There's little back roads and little towns sometimes I never heard of them. I start to expect the gas station attendants to know me when I arrive. I get excited that I've been there before. I want them to welcome me. I'm disappointed when they don't. Something that I don't want to be true starts lookin' like it's all that's true only I don't know what it is. No. No. I need my marriage. I come here to tell you. I got to stay married. I'm lost without her.

* * *

EDDIE: I feel awful.
[BONNIE: Whatsamatter?]
EDDIE: I dunno. I'm depressed.
[PHIL: What about?]
EDDIE: Everything. (*Gesturing, the newspaper still in* HIS *hand,* HE *notices it*) You read this shit. Look at this shit.
[PHIL: You depressed about the news, Eddie?]
EDDIE: Yeh.
[PHIL: You depressed about the newspaper?]
EDDIE: It's depressing. You read about this fucking neutron bomb? Look at this. (*Hands a part of the paper to* PHIL, *as* BONNIE *is inching nearer.* PHIL *sits on the arm of the couch, looking at the paper.* EDDIE, *clutching a part of the paper, is trying to stand*)
[PHIL: It's depressing. You depressed about the neutron bomb, Eddie?]
EDDIE: Yeah.
    There is an element here of hope in both BONNIE *and* PHIL *that*

EDDIE *may tell them something to explain, in fact, what's been going on.*

[BONNIE: It's depressing. *(Kneeling on the armchair, SHE looks over the back at EDDIE and PHIL with their newspapers)* The newspaper is very depressing. I get depressed every time I read it.]

EDDIE: I mean, not that I would suggest that, you know, the anxiety of this age is an unprecedented anxiety, but I'm fucking worried about it, you know. *(Taking a big drink, which empties the bottle HE has)*

[PHIL: So it's the newspaper and all the news got you down, huh, Eddie?]

EDDIE: *(Crossing with HIS tattered newspaper to the coffee table for another bottle sitting there):* I mean, the aborigine had a lot of problems—nobody is going to say he didn't—tigers in the trees, dogs after his food; and in the Middle Ages, there was goblins and witches in the woods. But this neutron bomb has come along and this sonofabitch has got this ATTITUDE. I mean, inherent in the conception of it is this fucking ATTITUDE about what is worthwhile in the world and what is worth preserving. And do you know what this fastidious prick has at the top of its hierarchy—what sits at the pinnacle? THINGS! *(HE takes a huge drink of vodka)* Put one down in the vicinity of this room and we're out. The three of us—out, out, out! "Well, I think I'll go downtown tomorrow and buy some new shoe—" WHACK! You're out! *(HE goes reeling toward the kitchen)* "Well, I thought I'd apologize for my reprehensible—" You're out! No shoes, no apologize. But guess what? The glasses don't even crack. *(HE has a glass)* The magazine's fine. The chairs, the table—*(HE knocks a chair over)* The phone'll ring if there's anybody to call. The things are unfucking disturbed. It annihilates people and saves THINGS. It loves things. It is a thing that loves things. Technology has found a way to save its own ass! And whether we know it or not, we KNOW it—that's eating at us. *(Lurching now HE grabs up a wastebasket, appears* *about to vomit in it, clutches it)* And where other, older, earlier people—the Ancients might have had some consolation from a view of the heavens as inhabited by this thoughtful, you know, meditative, maybe a trifle unpredictable and wrathful, but nevertheless UP THERE—this divine onlooker—*(Staggering about with* HIS *bottle and basket)*—we have bureaucrats devoted to the accumulation of incomprehensible data—we have connoisseurs of graft and the filibuster—virtuosos of the three-martini lunch for whom we vote on the basis of their personal appearance. The air's bad, the water's got poison in it, and into whose eyes do we find ourselves staring when we look for providence? We have emptied out the heavens and put oblivion in the hands of a bunch of aging insurance salesmen whose jobs are insecure. *(HE ends up leaning against the counter, the basket under* HIS *arm, the bottle in* HIS *hand.)*

THE INCREDIBLY FAMOUS WILLY RIVERS
Stephen Metcalfe

The present. A stage. WILLY RIVERS *(20s), a rock musician who was nearly killed by the assassination attempt of a crazed fan, tries to stage a comeback. Part of* HIS *effort is to recount the past events of* HIS *life that led to stardom. Here* HE *remembers* HIS *first gig.*

WILLY: My first gig, man, was in the high school gym. A battle of the bands. Aw, but we were ready. Me and my band even skipped a day of school that week to practice. Mom was going to go shopping. I kept calling home, waiting for her to leave so we could go over and jam. She'd answer, I'd hang up. Finally she didn't answer. We hit the house, turned the stereo on while we tuned up. Five minutes later cops barged in with drawn guns. Mom had freaked out about the phone calls, decided robbers were casing the joint. Cops had kept an open line on the place, bugged it.

We came in and blasted some sergeant into the ozone with Jimi Hendrix, Voodoo Child Slight Return. I got arrested in my own house. Had to do 26 hours of detention. But it was worth it. What dumb kids. We were. Fiddling with our amps that were no bigger than library books. Wa-wa pedal on loan. Four dollar fuzzbox. Feedback mikes. Test! One, two! *Wherraughhh!* The soundcheck was longer than our set. We only knew three songs but depending on the drum solo we could stretch'm anywhere from ten minutes to four hours. Playing. Rock and roll. And all the guys and the girls that we went to school with everyday, the jocks, the cheerleaders, the freaks, the beeries and the druggies, the grease eddies . . . everyone listening. Dancing. Bonded together by it. As into digging us as we were into playing for them. Man . . . what an innocent time. Playing for friends for free.

IT'S ONLY A PLAY   Terrence McNally

The present. The bedroom in a New York townhouse. An opening night party for a new play is in progress downstairs. TORCH, a dog, is growling and locked in the bathroom. JAMES WICKER (40s), an actor in a television series, comes in to use the telephone and calls HIS agent back in California.

JAMES: *(Into phone)* I'm sitting ten feet from a rabid dog who just bit Arlene Francis in the townhouse of a lady producer whose husband got mugged in the men's room at Sardi's. I will never knock California again. Where was I? Oh, the play! *(HE makes himself comfortable for a long haul on the telephone. HIS voice glows with relish)* Darling, what is your traditional Thanksgiving dinner? . . . Well this one is a thirty-five pound Butterball. Bob Fosse asked me what I thought at intermission and all I said was "Gobble, gobble" and he wet himself. Of course I don't want you to give that to Liz Smith. Are you crazy? I may want to work with these people. How was Jack Nimble? He was terrible, just terrible. But tell me this and tell me no more: when was he ever any good? All of my mannerisms and none of my warmth. Of course I would have been wonderful in it. It was written for me. And you want to hear the killer? I wasn't even mentioned in Peter's biography in the Playbill. I mean, let's face it. I did create the lead in his one and only hit but do you think I got so much as even a mention in his bio tonight? Well, that's a best friend for you. I fly in three thousand miles on the goddamn Red Eye for his opening and I'm not even mentioned in the goddamn Playbill. The egos in this business! What about Virginia Noyes? Terrible, just terrible. I haven't seen a performance like that since her last one. Well of course she wanted to come back to Broadway. After her last couple of pictures, she had to go somewhere. Terrible direction, just terrible. Boy wonder he may well be; the new Trevor Nunn he's not. He's not even the old Mike Nichols. Frank something. He's out of Chicago. Aren't they all? Sets? What sets? It took place on a goddamn tilted disk. Give me scenery or count me out. Hideous costumes. Darling, I would have made my first entrance in a leather codpiece and sort of antlers. I kid you not. There but for the grace of ABC went I. Darling, Arnold Schwarzenegger couldn't have held this one up. Oh, and guess who was sitting next to me at the theatre? Rita Moreno in a Day-Glo turban. She was with Calvin Klein. I wish you could have seen her face when he introduced her to Jean Kennedy as Chita Rivera! Who? Rita or Chita? Terrible, just terrible. But listen, darling, what do I know? What do any of us old gypsies know? I liked *The Rink*.

THE JAIL DIARY OF ALBIE SACHS
David Edgar

*The early 1960s. The cell of a prison in Cape Town, South Africa.
ALBIE SACHS (29), a young white South African lawyer and activist, is being held in solitary confinement to break HIS will and resistence. HIS diary records HIS thoughts during different stages of HIS six-month ordeal. In this episode, HE tries to decide what HE will write, novel or play.*

ALBIE: At first it was a book. But books are flat, controlled. The stuff of life is rolled up flat and sliced in two-dimensional pages. I wanted something more immediate, more active, more alive. So it had to be a play.

And working on the play is fighting back. The worse the things they do, the more I suffer, then the better, richer, deeper is the play.

(HE stands, growing in enthusiasm)

There will be singing, Africans will sing, to start the play. The play's in Africa. I see these cubes, they look opaque, in fact they are transparent, made of gauze, and they light up, you see people in them. Danny, me, the other 90-days. But first, the stage is dark. The singing. Then I come on—actually me, or someone who's made up to look like me—and I—or whoever's playing me—explains the play, that it is true, that this is what occurred. And then he's in the cell. He prods the walls, and says out loud, so this is what it's like.

The thoughts, perhaps, are pre-recorded, or the actor has a tiny microphone to whisper in.

Through him, we see his life, inside the cell. One scene, perhaps, will show me exercising, and the pain of it, and how it must be gone through. In another, there will be the caterpillar, and the draughts, the cleaning of my comb, the writing with the cheese, and, most of all, the singing. From my cube, from me, and the other cubes, the fact that isolation is the worst thing of them all, the crowd is not an enemy, the singing is an act of love.

And then perhaps I'll tell the audience—myself, or who is playing me—will tell the audience of how I thought that I would write a play, a play-within-a-play, or rather, a playwright within a play; and the play may even somewhere have the playwright writing it, and thinking of the opaque cubes, and working out the dialogue, and saying "this is what it's like," the playwright writes his play within the play.

But as I think of it, I am aware, increasingly, the real problem is to show just what it's like, in isolation, the disintegration, and the horror of it all, to people who are not alone, because they are together, watching, as an audience, my play.

And then, I think.

Perhaps the best thing is, not in the play, but in the audience, for them to see, for me to come out, to the audience, and say, my day is sitting staring at a wall, now I am going to make you sit and stare, you mustn't talk, or read your programmes, look at other people. For three minutes, you must sit and stare.

And then, perhaps, they'd know.

Just what it's like.

(Pause.

For about 15 seconds.

Then ALBIE *goes to his bunk.*

HE *lies down.*

Another three-quarters of a minute.

ALBIE *puts his forearms across his face.*

HE *does not move, for another minute and a half.*

Then HE *puts his arms by his side.*

Another half a minute.

Then HE *swings his legs out, stands.*

HE *speaks, not to the* AUDIENCE, *briskly, as* HE *walks out,*

through the fourth wall of the cell)

ALBIE: When this is over, I will leave South Africa. I owe that thing to me.

(ALBIE *walks out of the set, off the stage.*)

A KNIFE IN THE HEART   Susan Yankowitz

The present. A bedroom. DONALD HOLT, *an assassin, is standing in front of a full-length mirror in* HIS *underwear, holding a policeman's uniform in front of* HIM. *Beside* HIM *is a rack of clothing which holds suits and conventional clothing as well as uniforms of various sorts.*

DONALD: I'm a cop. Everyone in town knows me. I stand at an intersection and tell the traffic which way to go. Stop, I say. No, I don't even have to say it; I just hold up my hand. And the cars stop. Then what? Then I help the kids cross the street. Kids and old people. Then what? Then ... then ... someone starts running across the street against my command, he's got a scared look on his face. I bet he's a crook. I whip out my gun. Stop, I yell. He keeps running. He's a sneaky little guy with long legs. But I chase after him. Why? Why? Because it's my job. Stop, I shout, in the name of the law! That doesn't work. So what do I do? I let my gun shout for me. Bang bang bang. He sprawls out flat on the pavement. Then what happens? Then what? Then I grab the wallet from his hand, a wallet belonging to Mrs. Donenger, with her social security check already endorsed. Then what do I do? I bring the wallet back to Mrs. Donenger. Then what? Maybe she gives me ten bucks, which I'm not supposed to accept. Maybe she calls my mother, to tell her what a great guy I am, how I do my uniform proud. Then what?

(HE *is faltering now, as the story becomes anticlimactic, not bringing* HIM *to the peak of excitement and heroism* HE *craves*)

I guess I go back to directing traffic. No. No, that's not it. I go into ... into ... into ...

(flings down the policeman's uniform and picks up the soldier's motley camouflage)

... into the jungles, the forests, on my hands and knees. I'm searching for the enemy with my rifle and bayonet. I stab the bayonet spear into dead leaves; I'm getting in practice. Then I hear a noise behind me. I spin around—rat-a-tat-tat!—but after the sound clears, I don't see anybody, just trees that maybe aren't trees; everybody looks like a tree in war; even I do; that's my protection. Over my head planes are dropping big bundles—bombs or enemy people, I don't know which, they both make a scream when they fall—and I cover my head. I crouch down. It's so quiet I don't know where I am. The stars are like little candles ... But I can't sleep. Soldiers can't sleep ... Damn, that's not the way it goes. I don't want to be asleep. I don't have to be.

(gets inspired)

There's a fire, that's it, an enormous fire ...

(throws down the soldier's uniform and wraps a firefighter's coat around HIS shoulders, puts the hat on HIS head)

... I hear the alarm. It's shrilling in my head. The engines come shrieking out of the firehouse and there I am, on the running board with the rest of them, and we ride, we ride till we get there, it's a house, no, it's an apartment house, all forty stories ablaze, and we unwind the hoses from the spools, we lug them close, and on comes the water, so powerful it's like we got the ocean roaring through that hose. But that's not enough. Water doesn't do it. A man's needed to do it. There are people screaming from the top windows. I run through the flames and up the stairways. The smoke is in my lungs. I burst through a door into the corridor. There are bodies everywhere. I drag two kids under my arms like they were footballs and I run with them, I run back down the stairs and into the icy air. Here they are, here they are, I did it, I yell. These kids are saved, the only ones, and I did it. I saved them. Then what? My picture's in the paper. I saved two kids. Then what? What?

(frantically drops the fireman's outfit and puts on the surgeon's white gown)

—Then I save more. I keep on saving people. I take hearts from dead people and make them pump again for dying ones. I cut out cancers with my knife. I sew on severed limbs. What for? So people can walk, so they can pick up dishes with their hands or play the piano. What for? Then what? I keep on operating. There's an emergency a minute. Someone almost dies every minute. But I save them. Then what? Then what? Then what?

LES LIASONS DANGEREUSES
Christopher Hampton

Winter 1780s. The Paris salon of the MARQUISE DE MERTEUIL The VICOMTE DE VALMONT (30s-40s) bursts ebulliently into the room to announce that HE has finally been successful in HIS seduction of the married MADAME DE TOURVEL. Here HE begins to give details of the seduction to HIS former lover, the MARQUISE.

VALMONT: Success.

[MERTEUIL: At last]

VALMONT: But worth waiting for.

(MERTEUIL flashes a chilly look at him, but he's too exhilarated to notice)

[MERTEUIL: So it worked, your foolproof plan?]

VALMONT: Of course it wasn't foolproof, I was exaggerating to cheer myself up, but I did prepare the ground as carefully as I could. And I must say, considering these last few weeks my letters were all returned unopened, or rather my letter, since I simply placed it every other day in a fresh envelope, the result has been a genuine triumph. *(By this time, HE's taken a seat and HE pauses, beaming compla-*

cently at MERTEUIL*)*

[MERTEUIL: And the plan?]

VALMONT: I discovered, by intercepting her correspondence in the usual way, that she had very wisely decided to change her confidante and was pouring out all her inmost thoughts to my aunt. So very subtly, and aided by the fact I looked terminally exhausted as a result of my exertions with Cécile, I began to hint to my aunt that I was losing the will to live, knowing that this would be passed on. At the same time, I began corresponding with her confessor, an amiably dim-witted Cistercian, whom I more or less forced to arrange the meeting with her, in return for the privilege of being allowed to save my soul, a privilege he will now, poor man, be obliged to forgo. So, the threat of suicide, the promise of reform.

[MERTEUIL: I'm afraid I can't say I find that very original.]

VALMONT: Effective though.

[MERTEUIL: Tell me about it.]

VALMONT: Well, I arrived about six . . .

[MERTEUIL: Yes, I think you may omit the details of the seduction, they're never very enlivening: just describe the event itself.]

VALMONT: It was . . . unprecedented

[MERTEUIL: Really?]

VALMONT: It had a kind of charm I don't think I've ever experienced before. Once she'd surrendered, she behaved with perfect candour. Total mutual delirium: which for the first time ever with me outlasted the pleasure itself. She was astonishing. So much so that I ended by falling on my knees and pledging her eternal love. And do you know, at the time, and for several hours afterwards, I actually meant it!

[MERTEUIL: I see.]

VALMONT: It's extraordinary, isn't it?

A LIE OF THE MIND   Sam Shepard

*The present. The stage is several isolated areas that reveal the stark
dingy rooms of two different houses. These two monologues are
by the brothers* JAKE *(30s-40s) and* FRANKIE *(20s-30s). In the
first,* JAKE, *who has returned home after shooting* HIS *wife* BETH
in the head, tells FRANKIE *about* HIS *jealousy over* BETH's *acting
"career." In the second,* FRANKIE, *shot in the leg by* BETH's *father,* BAYLOR, *lies on the floor of* BAYLOR's *house in pain.*

JAKE: She was goin' to these goddamn rehearsals every day.
Every day. Every single day. Hardly ever see her. I saw enough
though. Believe you me. Saw enough to know somethin' was
goin' on.[. . .] *(Builds)* I'm no dummy. Doesn't take much to
put it together. Woman starts dressin' more and more skimpy every
time she goes out. Starts puttin' on more and more smells. Oils.
She was always oiling herself before she went out. Every morning.
Smell would wake me up. Coconut or Butterscotch or some goddamn thing. Sweet stuff. Youda thought she was an ice-cream
sundae. I'd watch her oiling herself while I pretended to be asleep.
She was in a dream, the way she did it. Like she was imagining
someone else touching her. Not me. Never me. Someone else.
[FRANKIE: Who?]
JAKE: *(Stands, moves around space, gains momentum)* Some
guy. I don't know. Some actor-jerk. I knew she was gettin' herself ready for him. I could tell. Got worse and worse. When I finally called her on it she denied it flat. I knew she was lying too.
Could tell it right away. The way she took it so light. Tried to cast
it off like it was nothin'. Then she starts tellin' me it's all in *my*
head. Some imaginary deal I'd cooked up in *my* head. Had nothin'
to do with her, she said. Made me try to believe I was crazy. She's
all innocent and I'm crazy. So I told her—I told her—I laid it on the
line to her. Square business. I says—no more high heels! No
more wearin' them high spiky high heels to rehearsals. No more a'

88

that shit. And she laughs. Right to my face. She laughs. Kept puttin' 'em on. Every mornin'. Puttin' 'em back on. She says it's right for the part. Made her feel like the character she says. Then I told her she had to wear a bra and she paid no attention to that either. You could see right through her damn blouse. Right clean through it. And she never wore underpants either. That's what really got me. No underpants. You could see everything.[. . .] *(Returns to speed, moves)* Okay. Then she starts readin' the lines with me, at night. In bed. Readin' the lines. I'm helpin' her out, right? Helpin' her memorize the damn lines so she can run off every morning and say 'em to some other guy. Day after day. Same lines. And these lines are all about how she's bound and determined to get this guy back in the sack with her after all these years he's been ignoring her. How she still loves him even though he hates her. How she's saving her body up for him and him only.

[FRANKIE: Well, it was just a play, wasn't it?]

JAKE: Yeah, a play. That's right. Just a play. "Pretend." That's what she said. "Just pretend." I know what they were doing! I know damn well what they were doin'! I know what that acting shit is all about. They try to "believe" they're the person. Right? Try to believe so hard they're the person that they actually think they become the person. So you know what that means don't ya?

[FRANKIE: What]

JAKE: They start doin' all the same stuff the person does!

[FRANKIE: What person?]

JAKE: The person! The—whad'ya call it? The—

[FRANKIE: Character?]

JAKE: Yeah. The character. That's right. They start acting that way in real life. Just like the character. Walkin' around—talkin' that way. You shoulda seen the way she started to walk and talk. I couldn't believe it. Changed her hair and everything. Put a wig on. Changed her clothes. Everything changed. She was unrecognizable. I didn't even know who I was with anymore. I told her. I told her, look—"I don't know who you think you are now but I'd just as soon you come on back to the real world here." And you know what she tells me?

[FRANKIE: What?]

JAKE:She tells me this is the real world. This acting shit is more real than the real world to her. Can you believe that? And she was tryin' to convince me that *I* was crazy?

* * *

FRANKIE: Hey look! Hey! I've got a bullet hole in my leg! All right? I've got a bullet hole clean through my leg! And you did it! And it's not gettin' any better. It's gettin' worse, in fact. So don't try to scare me with this stuff about lawyers, because I'm not buyin' it. I've got a serious injury here!

[BAYLOR: Aw, stop complainin', will ya. I've had a belly full a' complaints in this house.]

FRANKIE: Look—I don't know why it is but nobody around here will make any effort to try and get me outa here. How come that is? My brother—I've got a brother with a real short fuse. He gets weird ideas in his head. It doesn't take much to tip him over the edge. Now I've been here way too long. Way, way past the time I was supposed to get back. And he's gonna start gettin' the wrong idea about me and your daughter. I mean, your daughter is his wife. You know that, don't ya? I mean I suppose you know that but it's hard to tell anymore if anybody knows anything about anybody else around here. Like her, for instance. Your daughter. She is getting very strange with me. Very strange. I mean she started talkin' to me like I was him. Like I was my brother. To her, I mean. Like she thought I was him and not me. Your daughter. Beth. I mean I don't even know if she knows who I am anymore but—she thinks—she thinks her brother—your son and you, in fact—even you—she includes you in this too—she thinks you and

90

him, your son and you, are somehow responsible for taking her brain out. For removing her brain. Did you know about all this?

LYDIE BREEZE   John Guare

It is 1895. The Hickman House on Nantucket Island in the summer. LUCIAN ROCK (30s), a nattily dressed inventor, suddenly appears at the door of the house to ask JOSHUA HICKMAN if HE might have the hand of LYDIE HICKMAN in marriage. LUCIAN speaks as quickly as one of HIS high speed sewing machines, and HE disappears as abruptly as HE appears.

MAN'S VOICE: *(Offstage.)* Mr. Hickman! *(Gussie ducks out of the room as a nattily dressed man appears on the porch. His name is Lucian Rock)*
LUCIAN: Mr. Hickman?
[JOSHUA: Yes? *(Lucian enters.)*]
LUCIAN: I have to come this early as I'm leaving later this afternoon. May I come in?
[JOSHUA: You've already done that.]
LUCIAN: Now how can I put this?
[JOSHUA: I don't do business with people who lack a name.]
LUCIAN: I am nervous. My palms are ice. My knees are gelatin.
[JOSHUA: Your palms are ice. Your knees are gelatin. I'm glad each of them has a little name. Now what's your name?]
LUCIAN: Lucian Rock. *(Lucian offers Joshua his card)*
[JOSHUA: *(Reads)* Lucian Rock, Inventor. Oh! You're the inventor! Here for the summer. I read about you in the newspaper.]
LUCIAN: Yes, I'm the inventor. A high speed version of the sewing machine adapted for industrial use. May I sit down? The other day I saw a beautiful young girl in town. How extraordinary to see Aphrodite window-shopping in a summer resort. I followed her down a dark corridor. I felt her soul was calling to my soul.

Please, my flights of poetry are indicative of my interior emotional state. I felt I had entered a dark temple for I saw scores of tiny silver lights glowing. The giggling I heard made me realize it was merely street toughs holding fireflies captive in milk bottles. A match was struck, a fuse was lit, dropped into the milk bottle. An explosion. The children shrieked. Shattered glass. This stellar member of the distaff sex reached her hand to her eyes. And this Dido, this Persephone ran out the dark back door into the bright light of mythology. But I refuse to let her exist in antiquities of my heart—I've been practicing these words so I have to go at this pace. I'm going off to Europe, sailing to England tomorrow at midnight. My high speed sewing machines adapted for industrial use are being presented at various major courts of those aforesaid countries. And would like on my arm—I didn't practice this part well enough, I have been in my laboratories in Schenectady, New York—On my arm the most beautiful young creature, as I said, a Persephone. I inquired of various personages in town. Ahhh, the Hickman girl, Doctor Paynter said.

[JOSHUA: This is the God damndest thing I . . .]

LUCIAN: Now wait. I'm not asking you to hand your daughter over to me today. I will marry your daughter, tomorrow. I will make all financial arrangements. We will be married in Boston. We will sail to Europe where she'll be meeting Princes of Wales and Princesses of France. And of course the Hapsburgs and all those Balkans. Up into Saint Petersburg. I know I'm an early caller and your daughter must be upstairs sleeping. I'll walk down to the beach. Tramp along the sea. Expand my lungs. Prepare my farewell to America. Prepare myself for your daughter's answer.

MA RAINEY'S BLACK BOTTOM

August Wilson

1927. Chicago. The backroom of a small-time recording studio where the famous MA RAINEY is recording a record. During a rehearsal break, TOLEDO (60s), a black pianist, tells three other side musicians about the black man's origins and plight in a white world. Since they've all been having a bite to eat, HE uses the image of a stew to cook-up a homespun allegory. In the second monologue, a bit further in the action, LEVEE (32), a jazz trumpeter with ambitions, lashes out at the older musicians and expresses HIS scorn and anger towards the white man. HE reveals what happened to HIM as a child in Tennessee.

TOLEDO: Now, I'm gonna show you how this goes . . . where you just a leftover from history. Everybody come from different places in Africa, right? Come from different tribes and things. Soonawhile they began to make one big stew. You had the carrots, the peas, and potatoes and whatnot over here. And over there you had the meat, the nuts, the okra, corn . . . and then you mix it up and let it cook right through to get the flavors flowing together . . . then you got one thing. You got a stew.

Now you take and eat the stew. You take and make your history with that stew. All right. Now it's over. Your history's over and you done ate the stew. But you look around and you see some carrots over here, some potatoes over there. That stew's still there. You done made your history and it's still there. You can't eat it all. So what you got? You got some leftovers. That's what it is. You got leftovers and you can't do nothing with it. You already making you another history . . . cooking you another meal, and you don't need them leftovers no more. What to do?

See, we's the leftovers. The colored man is the leftovers. Now, what's the colored man gonna do with himself? That's what we waiting to find out. But first we gotta know we the leftovers.

Now, who knows that? You find me a nigger that knows that and I'll turn any whichaway you want me to. I'll bend over for you. You ain't gonna find that. And that's what the problem is. The problem ain't with the white man. The white man knows you just a leftover. 'Cause he the one who done the eating and he know what he done ate. But we don't know that we been took and made history out of. Done went and filled the white man's belly and now he's full and tired and wants you to get out the way and let him be by himself. Now, I know what I'm talking about. And if you wanna find out, you just ask Mr. Irvin what he had for supper yesterday. And if he's an honest white man . . . which is asking for a whole heap of a lot . . . he'll tell you he done ate your black ass and if you please I'm full up with you . . . so go on and get off the plate and let me eat something else.

* * *

LEVEE: Levee got to be Levee! And he don't need nobody messing with him about the white man—cause you don't know nothing about me. You don't know Levee. You don't know nothing about what kind of blood I got! What kind of heart I got beating here!

(HE *pounds his chest*)

I was eight years old when I watched a gang of white mens come into my daddy's house and have to do with my mama any way they wanted.

(*Pauses*)

We was living in Jefferson County, about eighty miles outside of Natchez. My daddy's name was Memphis . . . Memphis Lee Green . . . had him near fifty acres of good farming land. I'm talking about good land! Grow anything you want! He done gone off of shares and bought this land from Mr. Hallie's widow woman after he done passed on. Folks called him an uppity nigger 'cause he done saved and borrowed to where he could buy this land and be

94

independent.

(Pauses)

It was coming on planting time and my daddy went into Natchez to get him some seed and fertilizer. Called me, say, "Levee you the man of the house now. Take care of your mama while I'm gone." I wasn't but a little boy, eight years old.

(Pauses)

My mama was frying up some chicken when them mens come in that house. Must have been eight or nine of them. She standing there frying that chicken and them mens come and took hold of her just like you take hold of a mule and make him do what you want.

(Pauses)

There was my mama with a gang of white mens. She tried to fight them off, but I could see where it wasn't gonna do her any good, I didn't know what they were doing to her . . . but I figured whatever it was they may as well do to me too. My daddy had a knife that he kept around there for hunting and working and whatnot. I knew where he kept it and I went and got it.

I'm gonna show you how spooked up I was by the white man. I tried my damndest to cut one of them's throat! I hit him on the shoulder with it. He reached back and grabbed hold of that knife and whacked me across the chest with it.

(LEVEE raises his shirt to show a long ugly scar)

That's what made them stop. They was scared I was gonna bleed to death. My mama wrapped a sheet around me and carried me two miles down to the Furlow place and they drove me up to Doc Albans. He was waiting on a calf to be born, and say he ain't had time to see me. They carried me up to Miss Etta, the midwife, and she fixed me up.

My daddy came back and acted like he done accepted the facts of what happened. But he got the names of them mens from mama. He found out who they was and then we announced we was moving out of that county. Said good-bye to everybody . . . all the neighbors. My daddy went and smiled in the face of one of them crackers who had been with my mama. Smiled in his face and sold him our land. We moved over with relations in Caldwell. He got us settled in and then he took off one day. I ain't never seen him since. He sneaked back, hiding up in the woods, laying to get them eight or nine men.

(Pauses)

He got four of them before they got him. They tracked him down in the woods. Caught up with him and hung him and set him afire.

(Pauses)

My daddy wasn't spooked up by the white man. Nosir! and that taught me how to handle them. I seen my daddy go up and grin in this cracker's face . . . smile in his face and sell him his land. All the while he's planning how he's gonna get him and what he's gonna do to him. That taught me how to handle them. So you all just back up and leave Levee alone about the white man. I can smile and say yessir to whoever I please. I got time coming to me. You all just leave Levee alone about the white man.

MARCO POLO SINGS A SOLO   John Guare

1999. A surrealistic Norway of the future. The set of a film being made about Marco Polo. STONY, *the film's director and the center of the play's action, has been listening to* DIANE, HIS *wife,* TOM *and* LARRY *talk about a production they have just seen of Ibsen's play,* DOLL HOUSE, *directed by the son of Ingmar Bergman.* STONY *contradicts them on the details of Ibsen's play.*

[DIANE: The actors played *Doll House* entirely on trampolines. Nora doesn't just walk out the door, she leapt this incredible bounce into freedom. Into infinity. Stony, it was done by Ingmar Bergman's son and I thought of all these great men surpassing their fathers.

96

TOM: I'll set up the film, Diane.

LARRY: I've set up the film, Diane. *(The film begins. We hear the soundtrack: "Jordin, Jordin.")*]

STONY: Isn't it incredible. Here it is 1999 and people still miss the point of that play.

[TOM: And what is the point of the play?]

STONY: Nora never left.

[TOM: Pardon me while I laugh, but the entire point of the play is . . .]

STONY: Nora never left. Ibsen's entire point is Nora's husband knew she was leaving and quick as a shooting star, he constructed a new living room that enclosed the outside of the front door. So when Nora left she found herself not in the outside world, but in another, a newer, a stranger room. And since there was no door in that room, she drew a window and quickly climbed out of it. But her brilliant, heroic husband built a new room off that window. And she beat down the walls of that new room and the walls crumbled and her hands bled and the dust cleared and she found herself in a newer room still damp from construction. And she crawled through the ceiling, gnawing, and her husband dropped a new room on top of that escape hatch. So the wife invented fire and burned down all the rooms and her skin blistered but she smiled for she knew she would soon be free. And the smoke cleared and an enormous igloo domed the sky and she ripped out her heart and intestines and forged them into an ice pick and chopped her way out through the sky and she opened the ice door that would lead her into the nebula, the Milky Way, heaven, freedom, but no, she chopped back the door to heaven and was warmed by the glow of a cozy room, her Christmas card list, a lifetime subscription to a glossy magazine called *Me,* her children, her closet crammed with clothes, her possessions, her life sat waiting for her in a rocking chair.

THE MARRIAGE OF BETTE AND BOO
Christopher Durang

1960s. A middle class household in New Jersey. MATTHEW
HUDLOCKE *("SKIPPY"), addresses the audience as an adult narrator and plays* HIS *past self at different points in the play's action.
Here* HE *writes a student essay, integrating* HIS *troubled parents
into the fabric of a Thomas Hardy novel. In the second monologue,
a Catholic priest,* FATHER DONNALLY *(40s), lectures*
MATTHEW's *parents,* BETTE *and* BOO, *during a marriage retreat.*
HE *keeps digressing from a main point which* HE *doesn't seem to
know too much about anyway.*

MATT: *My Very Favorite Movie,* an essay by Matthew Hudlocke.
My very favorite movie . . . are . . . *Nights of Cabiria, 8 1/2,
Citizen Kane, L'Avventura, The Seventh Seal, Persona, The Parent
Trap, The Song of Bernadette, Potemkin, The Fire Within, The
Bells of St. Mary's, The Singing Nun, The Dancing Nun, The Nun
on the Fire Escape Outside My window, The Nun That Caused the
Chicago Fire, The Nun Also Rises, The Nun Who Came to Dinner,
The Caucasian Chalk Nun, Long Day's Journey into Nun, None
But the Lonely Heart,* and *The Nun Who Shot Liberty Valance.*
Page two. In the novels of Thomas Hardy, we find a deep and
unrelieved pessimism. Hardy's novels, set in his home town of
Wessex, contrast nature outside of man with the human nature
inside of man, coming together inexorably to cause human catastro-
phe. The sadness in Hardy—his lack of belief that a benevolent
God watches over human destiny, his sense of the waste and frustration of the average human life, his forceful irony in the face of
moral and metaphysical questions—is part of the late Victorian
mood. We can see something like it in A.E. Housman, or in
Emily's life. Shortly after Skippy's birth, Emily enters a convent,
but then leaves the convent due to nerves. Bette becomes pregnant
for the second time. Boo continues to drink. If psychiatrists had

98

existed in nineteenth-century Wessex, Hardy might suggest Bette and Boo seek counselling. Instead he has no advice to give them, and in 1886 he writes *The Mayor of Casterbridge*. This novel is one of Hardy's greatest successes, and Skippy studies it in college. When he is little, he studies *The Wind in the Willows* with Emily.

* * *

FATHER DONNALLY: In the name of the Father, of the Son, and of the Holy Ghost, Amen. Good evening, young marrieds. *(Looks about himself for a moment)* Am I in the right room?

[EMILY: I'm not married, Father. I hope you don't mind that I'm here.

FATHER DONNALLY: On the contrary. I'm delighted. I'm not married either. *(Laughs)*] The theme of marriage in the Catholic Church and in this retreat is centered around the story of Christ and the wedding feast at Cana. Jesus Christ blessed the young wedding couple at Cana, and when they ran out of expensive wine, He performed His first miracle—He took vats of water and He changed the water into wine. *(Holds up a glass)* I have some wine right here. *(Sips it)*

[BOO: *(To* BETTE*)* He drinks, Why don't you try to get him to stop drinking?

BETTE: Be quiet, Boo.]

FATHER DONNALLY: *(Laughs nervously)* Please don't talk when I'm talking. *(Starts* HIS *speech)* Young marrieds have many problems to get used to. For some of them this is the first person of the opposite sex the other has ever known. The husband may not be used to having a woman in his bathroom. The wife may not be used to a strong masculine odor in her boudoir. Or then the wife may not cook well enough. How many marriages have floundered on the rocks of ill-cooked bacon? *(Pause)* I used to amuse friends by imitating bacon in a saucepan. Would anyone like to see that? *(HE looks around. Joan, Karl, and Soot raise their hands. After a mo-*

ment, EMILY, *rather confused raises* HER *hand also.* FATHER DONNALLY *falls to the ground and does a fairly good—or if not good, at least unabashedly peculiar—imitation of bacon, making sizzling noises and contorting* HIS *body to represent becoming crisp. Toward the end,* HE *makes sputtering noises into the air. Then* HE *stands up again. All present applaud with varying degrees of approval or incredulity.)* I also do coffee percolating. (HE *does this)* Pt. Pt. Ptptptptptptptptpt. Bacon's better. But things like coffee and bacon are important in a marriage, because they represent things that the wife does to make her husband happy. Or fat. *(Laughs)* The wife cooks the bacon, and the husband brings home the bacon. This is how St. Paul saw marriage, although they probably didn't really eat port back then, the curing process was not very well worked out in Christ's time, which is why so many of them followed the Jewish dietary laws even though they were Christians. I know I'm glad to be living now when we have cured pork and plumbing and showers rather than back when Christ lived. Many priests say they wish they had lived in Christ's time so they could have met Him; that would, of course, have been very nice, but I'm glad I live now and that I have a shower.

MOTEL CHRONICLES   Sam Shepard

MOTEL CHRONICLES *is a collection of short autobiographical writings by* SAM SHEPARD. *Both of these selections are reminiscences of childhood and require no particular background to perform.*

What I saw was this: From a distance. Four of them. Moving like snakes. Dragging their legs toward the black herd. Like their legs were dead. Pulling their brown bellies across stone. I didn't even recognize them as human at first. Least of all Sioux. I thought they might be dark dogs or something. Deep holes in the prairie. Moving. I couldn't stop watching them move. I wasn't afraid. I knew the wagons were getting farther away. I knew I was being left behind. But I wasn't afraid. I watched them leap. All four of them at once. They dragged the big bull down. Ripped open the neck with their knives. Ripped open the belly. The belly fell out on the prairie. The membrane broke. All the insides rolled out, steaming in the grass. My eyes began to sting. I heard them singing. Not really a song. A kind of screaming as they tore out the tongue and ate it between them. The bull still twitching. Thin columns of dust rose up and I followed the dust with my eyes. The Tetons loomed behind. All blue. And I watched those mountains glow. And I thought about Boston. And I missed my piano. And I couldn't believe my piano was in the same world, living in the same time and I'd never see Boston again.

7/17/80
San Anselmo, Ca.

* * *

My Dad had this habit of picking at a shrapnel scar on the back of his neck every time he heard a plane go over our land. He'd be stooped over in the orchard repairing the irrigation pipes or the tractor and he'd hear a plane then slowly straighten up, peel off his straw Mexican hat, run his hand through his hair, wipe the sweat off on his thigh, hold the hat out in front of his forehead to shade his eyes, squint deep into the sky, fix the plane with one eye and begin picking slowly at the back of his neck. Just stare and pick. The scar was the mark of a World War II mission over Italy. A tiny piece of metal remained embedded just under the surface. What got me was the reflexive nature of this picking gesture. Every time he heard a plane he went for the scar. And he didn't stop picking at it until he'd identified the aircraft to his complete satisfaction. He delighted mostly in prop planes and this was the Fifties so there were quite a few big prop planes still in the air. If a formation of P-51's

went over, he would almost climb an Avocado tree with ecstasy.
Each identification was marked by a distinct emotional tone in his
voice. There were planes that had let him down in the heat of combat and he would spit in their direction. On the other hand, a B-54
got a somber, almost religious tone. Usually just the minimal code
number was uttered: "B-54," he would say, then, satisfied, he
would drag his eyes back down to earth and return to his work. It
seemed odd to me how a man who loved the sky so much could also
love the land.

8/29/80
Santa Rosa, Ca.

MY DINNER WITH ANDRÉ
Wallace Shawn & André Gregory

*The present. A New York restaurant where a wide-ranging conver-
sation between* ANDRÉ *(40s), an experimental theatre director, and*
WALLY *(30s), an off-Broadway playwright, is underway. The
frustrations that* BOTH *feel towards other people and* THEIR *profession, the theatre, begins to intensify and leave* THEM *searching
for words and answers. First* WALLY *has* HIS *say and then*
ANDRÉ *replies.*

WALLY: And I mean, when Debby was working as a secretary,
you know, if she would tell people what she did, they would just go
insane. I mean, they just wouldn't be able to handle it. You know,
it would be as if she'd said—uh—"Well, you know, I'm serving a
life sentence for child murdering." And I mean, you know, when
you talk about our attitudes toward people—I mean, you know, I
think of myself as a very decent, good person simply because I
think I'm reasonably friendly to most of the people I happen to meet
every day. I mean, I really think of myself quite smugly, and I
think I'm a perfectly nice guy, so long as I somehow think of the

102

world as consisting of, you know, just the small circle of the people I know as friends—or just the few people that we know in this little world of our hobbies—the theatre or whatever it is. And I'm really quite self-satisfied. I'm happy with myself. I have no complaint about myself. I mean, if I'm just one more nice student in the Dalton School in the seventh grade, well then, you know, I'm just as nice as the next guy in the seventh grade. But the thing is, you know, let's face it, there's a whole enormous world out there that I don't ever think about, and I *certainly* don't take responsibility for how I've lived in *that* world. I mean, if I were actually to confront the fact that I'm sort of sharing this stage with the starving person in Africa somewhere, well then I wouldn't feel so great about myself. So naturally I blot those people out of my perception. So of course I'm ignoring a whole section of the real world. You know, Hannah Arendt was always writing about the fact that the more involved you are in corruption or evil, and the more areas of your own existence there are that you therefore don't want to think about, or that you can't face, or that you have to lie about, the more distorted your perception of reality will be in general. *(Pause)* In other words, we all have every reason to hide from reality, and it's a terrible problem. But I mean, frankly, when I write a play, in a way one of the things I guess I'm trying to do is precisely to bring myself up against some little bits of reality, and I'm trying to share that with an audience. *(Pause. ANDRÉ says nothing)* I mean, the theatre—I mean, of course we all know that the theatre is in terrible shape today. I mean, you know, at least a few years ago people who really cared about the theatre used to say, "The theatre is dead." But now everyone has redefined the theatre in such a trivial way. You know, I mean, I know people who are involved with the theatre who go to see things now that—I mean, a few years ago these same people would have just been *embarrassed* to have even *seen* some of these plays—I mean, they would have just *shrunk,* you know, just in *horror,* at the superficiality of these things. But *now* they say, "Oh, that was pretty good." It's just incredible. And I just find that attitude unbearable, because I actually do believe that the theatre can be very important—it can actually help people come in contact with reality. Now you may not feel that at all. You may find that absurd.

* * *

ANDRÉ: Well, Wally, how do you think if affects an audience to put on one of these plays in which you show that people are totally isolated now, and they can't reach others, and their lives are obsessive and driven and desperate? Or how does it affect them to see a play that shows that our world is full of nothing but shocking sexual events and violence and terror? Does that help to wake up a sleeping audience? You see, I don't think so, because I think it's very likely that the picture of the world that you're showing them in a play like that is exactly the picture of the world that they have already. You know, they *know* their own lives and relationships are painful and difficult, and if they watch the evening news on television, well there what they see is a terrifying chaotic universe full of rapes and murders and hands cut off by subway cars and children pushing their parents out of windows. So the play simply tells them that their impression of the world is correct, and there's absolutely no way out, there's nothing they can do. They end up feeling passive and impotent. And so the experience has helped to deaden them. They're more asleep than when they went into the theatre. I mean, I love the theatre, Wally, I want to direct plays again, but it's very difficult, because the things that I'd like to do in the theatre . . . I mean, look at something like that christening that my group arranged for me in the forest in Poland. Well, there was an example of people creating something that really had all the elements of theatre. It was worked on carefully, it was thought about carefully, it was done with exquisite taste and magic, and they in fact created something—which in this case was in a way just for an audience of one, just for me—they in fact created something that had ritual, love,

104

surprise, denouement, beginning, middle, and end—and it had a
real moon instead of a painted moon and a real castle instead of a
painted castle, but it was an incredibly beautiful piece of theatre.
And the impact it had on its audience, on me, was somehow a totally
positive one. It didn't deaden me, it brought me to life.

NATIVE SPEECH   Eric Overmyer

*Perhaps the present. An underground radio station set in a
devastated neighborhood. Outside, a darkening world. Dangerous.
Always winter. HUNGRY MOTHER (late 30s), a white disk jockey, is a shambly, disheveled man. This is HIS final speech of the
play. It's effect is like dial switching.*

HUNGRY MOTHER: *(Into the mike)* Test if it dead . . . Give
me a try before you pass me by . . . Close enough for ground
zero . . . I've got some good phrases from romantic literature in
my head. It's too bad . . . This is the Hungry Mother. The Uni-
versal Disc Jockey. God's own deejay. Goin' down slow. *(Black)*
Cat's pajamas . . . This is your Hungry Mother talkin' to you! I
cannot be slow—that why I'm so fast! *(Sings an offhand blues)*
Goin' down slow—oh goin' down slow—but at least I am—going'
down—on yoouuu. *(Laid back Top 40)* One of our very very large
numbers, I just know you're gonna love this one—an old old stand-
bye, a super-monster in its time—an antediluvian smash—*Sweet
Gash!* Oh so sweet! Play it for me just one more time.

  (Frenzied Top 40) Get down! As your audio agitator I strongly
advise you to get down! Get Down! Work yourselves into a frenzy
with—Screaming Annie! *(A series of gagging screams. Then in the
grand manner)* When men were men and rock and roll was king.
Never the twain shall meet. Send a salami to your boy in the army.
(Slight pause) Talking heads. Runs on lethargy. Human freedom
diminishing, even vanishing. Ruination.

(Mellifluous) We'll have the latest up-to-date quotations on—human wreckage futures in a moment. *(Beat)* This is your favorite Hungry Mother, illuminating the dark contours of native speech. *(Pause. From this point on, the various radio voices drop away)*

Fuck. Fuck it. Fucked up. Hit you across your fucking mouth. Fuck with me and I'll really fuck you up . . . I try to watch my language, but I'm a victim of history. Or is it eschatology? Verbal inflation is at an all-time high. *(Slight pause)* First Chinese Baptist Church of the Deaf. *(Slight pause)* Social engineering. Upward mobility. *Stiletto. (Slight pause. A travel agent)* Vacation in—steamy—South Africa! *(Slight pause)* Say *hungry.*

(Slight pause. Cheery salesman) Death Boy, Brown Bomber, White Death, Stallion Stick, Casa Boom, Snow Storm, Allah Supreme, White Noise, Sweet Surrender, Death Wish, Turkish Delight! Any size lot, any cut ratio, buy in bulk and saaaave! If we don't have it, it ain't worth having! If our sauce don't send you, you got no place to go!

(Laughs, then screaming) That junk is shit! Shit! Stay 'way. Mother advises you to stay a-way—lay off it all 'cept for Death Wish Smoking Mixture Number 3. After all—why stick when you can blow? *(Slight pause)* Stick with us. *(Laughs)* Stick *with* us. Stick with *us.* Stick it. *(Slight pause)* Twenty-four hour shooting galleries. *(Slight pause)* The American Meat Institute presents. Our Lady Of The Cage

A new barbed-wire ballet. With automatic weapons. *(Slight pause)* Say hungry . . . I'm interested in abused forms. *(Black)* She not only willing, she *able.* Bevy. Doctor Feelgood. *(Sportsaster)* Playing hurt. Photo finish. Cut to ribbons . . . That goes without saying. *(Slight pause)* Dead on my feet. *(Slight pause)* I pay lip service every chance I get. Flophouse of Stalinism. Two mules and a colored boy. Better a cocksucker than a Communist. *(Pause)* Down avenues of blue exhaust. *(Pause)* Voodoo kit. Razor ribbon. Front me 'til Friday. A day late and a dollar short. Tryin' to get over. *(Pause)* Spike that beautiful black vein! Spike it! *(Pause)* Say *hungry!* . . . Born to shoot junk. Strafe me, baby. Strafe me. Up against it. *Aphasia*. All the rage. Hungry. Riff. On the rag. In the name of the father, and of the son, and of the holocaust. World without end. Shit from shortcake. Ecstatic suffering.

(HE *falters)* I disremember. *(Slight pause. Trembling)* Brush fire wars. Bane of my existence. Blue sky *ventures! (Top 40 outburst)* The watchword for today—*hydrogenize slumism!* Bear that in mind. *(Pause)* Under the gun. *(Pause)* Under the gun. *(Pause)* Under the gun. *(Pause)* Fre-fire zone. *(Pause)* When I get back . . . When I get back to The World—*(Lightly)* I ain't gonna do nothin' . . . but stay black—an' *die. (Slight pause)* I'm *serious. (Laughs. Freezes.)*

THE NORMAL HEART   Larry Kramer

February 1983. New York City. The crowded offices of a gay organization, hastily set-up to lobby support for the AIDS *health crisis.* NED WEEKS *(30s-40s), a writer who has been investigating the crisis and exposing the wholesale lack of alarm towards it by city officials, is told by* BRUCE NILES *(30s) details about the death of a friend,* ALBERT. *In the second monologue, two months later,* BRUCE *has told* NED *that* HIS *stories are causing trouble and hysteria.* NED *is asked to leave the organization* HE *helped found.* HE *reacts angrily to* BRUCE's *lack of fight and leadership.*

BRUCE: Ned, Albert is dead.[. . .] Do you know why? Because of me. Because he knows I'm so scared I'm some sort of carrier. This makes three people I've been with who are dead. I went to Emma and I begged her: please test me somehow, please tell me if I'm giving this to people. And she said she couldn't, there isn't any way they can find out anything because they still don't know what they're looking for. Albert, I think I loved him best of all, and he went so fast. His mother wanted him back in Phoenix before he died, this was last week when it was obvious, so I get permission from Emma and bundle him all up and take him to the plane in an ambulance. The pilot wouldn't take off and I refused to leave the plane—you would have been proud of me—so finally they get another pilot. Then, after we take off, Albert loses his mind, not recognizing me, not knowing where he is or that he's going home, and then, right there, on the plane, he becomes . . . incontinent. He starts doing it in his pants and all over the seat; shit, piss, everything. I pulled down my suitcase and yanked out whatever clothes were in there and I start mopping him up as best I can, and all these people are staring at us and moving away in droves and . . . I ram all these clothes back in the suitcase and I sit there holding his hand, saying, "Albert, please, no more, hold it in, man, I beg you, just for us, for Bruce and Albert." And when we got to Phoenix, there's a police van waiting for us and all the police are in complete protective rubber clothing, they looked like fucking astronauts, and by the time we got to the hospital where his mother had fixed up his room real nice, Albert was dead.

(NED *starts toward him*)

Wait. It gets worse. The hospital doctors refused to examine him to put a cause of death on the death certificate, and without a death certificate the undertakers wouldn't take him away, and neither would the police. Finally, some orderly comes in and stuffs Albert in a heavy-duty Glad Bag and motions us with his finger to follow and he puts him out in the back alley with the garbage. He says, "Hey, man. See what a big favor I've done for you, I got him out, I want fifty bucks." I paid him and then his mother and I carried the bag to her car and we finally found a black undertaker who cremated him for a thousand dollars, no questions asked.

(NED *crosses the* BRUCE *and embraces him;* BRUCE *puts his arms around* NED)

BRUCE: Would you and Felix mind if I spent the night on your sofa? Just one night. I don't want to go home.

* * *

NED: I belong to a culture that includes Proust, Henry James, Tchaikovsky, Cole Porter, Plato, Socrates, Aristotle, Alexander the Great, Michaelangelo, Leonardo da Vinci, Christopher Marlowe, Walt Whitman, Herman Melville, Tennessee Williams, Byron, E.M. Forster, Lorca, Auden, Francis Bacon, James Baldwin, Harry Stack Sullivan, John Maynard Keynes, Dag Hammarskjold . . . These are not invisible men. Poor Bruce. Poor frightened Bruce. Once upon a time you wanted to be a soldier. Bruce, did you know that it was an openly gay Englishman who was as responsible as any man for winning the Second World War? His name was Alan Turing and he cracked the Germans' Enigma code so the Allies knew in advance what the Nazis were going to do—and when the war was over he committed suicide he was so hounded for being gay. Why don't they teach any of this in the schools? If they did, maybe he wouldn't have killed himself and maybe you wouldn't be so terrified of who you are. The only way we'll have real pride is when we demand recognition of a culture that isn't just sexual. It's all there—all through history we've been there; but we have to claim it, and identify who was in it, and articulate what's in our minds and hearts and all our creative contributions to this earth. And until we do that, and until we organize ourselves block by neighborhood by city by state into a united visible community that fights back, we're doomed. That's how I want to be defined: as one of the men who fought the war. Being defined by our cocks is literally killing us. Must we all be reduced to becoming our own murderers? Why couldn't you and I, Bruce Niles and Ned Weeks, have been leaders in creating a new definition of what it means to be gay? I blame myself as much as you. Bruce, I know I'm an asshole. But, please, I beg you, don't shut me out.

ONE FOR THE ROAD
Harold Pinter

The present. A room. Morning. NICHOLAS *(30s-40s) at* HIS *desk.* HE *leans forwards and speaks into a machine.*

NICHOLAS:

Bring him in.

*(*HE *sits back. The door opens.* VICTOR *walks in, slowly.* HIS *clothes are torn.* HE *is bruised. The door closes behind him.*

Hello! Good morning. How are you? Let's not beat about the bush. Anything but that. *D'accord?* You're a civilized man. So am I. Sit down.

*(*VICTOR *slowly sits.* NICHOLAS *stands, walks over to him)*

What do you think this is? It's my finger. And this is my little finger. I wave my big finger in front of your eyes. Like this. And now I do the same with my little finger. I can also use both . . . at the same time. Like this. I can do absolutely anything I like. Do you think I'm mad? My mother did.

*(*HE *laughs)*

Do you think waving fingers in front of people's eyes is silly? I can see your point. You're a man of the highest intelligence. But would you take the same view if it was my boot—or my penis? Not my eyes. Other people's eyes. The eyes of people who are brought to me here. They're so vulnerable. The soul shines through them. Are you a religious man? I am. Which side do you think God is on? I'm going to have a drink.

*(*HE *goes to sideboard, pours whisky)*

You're probably wondering where your wife is. She's in another room.

*(*HE *drinks)*

Good-looking woman.

*(*HE *drinks)*

God, that was good.

*(*HE *pours another)*

110

Don't worry, I can hold my booze.

(HE drinks)

You may have noticed I'm the chatty type. You probably think I'm part of a predictable, formal, long-established pattern; i.e., I chat away, friendly, insouciant, I open the batting, as it were, in a light-hearted, even carefree manner, while another waits in the wings, silent, introspective, coiled like a puma. No, no. It's not quite like that. I run the place. God speaks through me. I'm referring to the Old Testament God, by the way, although I'm a long way from being Jewish. Everyone respects me here. Including you, I take it? I think that is the correct stance.

(Pause)

Stand up.

(VICTOR stands)

Sit down.

(VICTOR sits)

Thank you so much.

(Pause.)

OPEN ADMISSIONS   Shirley Lauro

The present. A New York City college speech class. CALVIN JEFFERSON (18), intense, intelligent, and street-smart, confronts HIS instructor GINNY CARLSEN about HIS grade, class performance and the value of what HE's being taught. Each of her responses deepens HIS anger and resentment.

CALVIN: But I don't know *how* to improve it. Thass what I come to ax *you!*

[GINNY: "Ask me," Calvin, "Ask me"!]

CALVIN: *(Furious now, backing her into chair)* "Ax you!?" Okay, man. Miss Shakespeare, Speech Communication I! Know what I'll "ax" you, how come I been in this here college all this time

and I don't know nothin more than when I came in? This supposed
to be some big break for me. Supposed to be my turn. You know
what I mean—an my sister Salina got me off the streets, man, where
I been dealing dope and been in six foster homes—and five schools,
she give me this break, 'cause I got brains! You know what I am
communicatin to you. Ever school I been has tole me I got brains
and can make somethin outa myself if I gits me the chance! This
here supposed to be it! Only nothin is happenin to me in my head
except I is gittin more and more confuse about what I knows and
what I don't know! So what I wanna "ax" you is: How come you
don't sit down with me and give me somethin I can "identify", and
teach me about it an how to git them big ideas down instead a givin
me a "B" an Franklin a "B". An Doreen a "B". What's that "B"
standin for, cause it surely ain't standin for no piece a work!

ORPHANS   Lyle Kessler

*The present. An old North Philadelphia row house owned by the
brothers TREAT (20s-30s) and PHILLIP. TREAT brings home
HAROLD (40s), a well-dressed businessman from Chicago, who is
first held captive and then takes over the running of the house once
HE is freed. In the first monologue, HAROLD tells TREAT about
FRED, another orphan HE knew back in Chicago. In the second
monologue, TREAT torments PHILLIP with a story about Errol
Flynn. HE uses the opportunity to destroy HIS brother's illusions.*

HAROLD: He was an orphan, just like me. We were newsboys
together, south side of Chicago. Little motherless newsboys standing in the cold, yelling "EXTRA! EXTRA! READ ALL ABOUT
IT!", fighting our way from the outskirts of the city to the very heart
of Chicago . . . Little motherless fucking orphans fighting tooth
and nail, block after block, fighting for each and every corner.
That's the free enterprise system, Treat. That's Capitalism!

(PHILLIP *sits on the floor, listening to the story.*) We use to watch the Dead End Kids together every Sunday matinee. He died of pneumonia though, one frigid January day. Freezing wind coming off the Lake. I had a Chicago Tribune tucked away inside my front shirt and one in my back. That's an old newsboys' trick, protects you from the elements. Only thing is on this particular day Fred sold the Tribune covering his chest. I told him he was crazy, temperature was dropping rapidly. He turned around and sold the other Tribune covering his back. Moderation, Treat, moderation! Poor motherless newsboy, totally exposed on that frigid January day. Had a hacking cough by the time we got back to the Orphanage. Later on a raging fever—the next morning he was gone[. . .] We buried him in the Orphans' Cemetery. I'm giving you a lesson in moderation, boys, and also economics, the profit motive. How far a man will go for financial gain. (HAROLD *crosses behind* TREAT *and puts his hand on his shoulder.* TREAT *pulls away.* HAROLD *stares at him a moment, picks up his drink and crosses to the window seat.* HE *looks out the window.*)

* * *

TREAT: I SAID I JUST NOW SEEN A FRIEND OF YOURS! (PHILLIP *returns with an empty large bottle of Hellman's Mayonnaise.* HE *places the flowers inside.*)
[PHILLIP: Who'd you see?]
TREAT: I seen an old re-run of the *Charge of the Light Brigade*, starring none other than your old buddy, Errol Flynn.
[PHILLIP: He's not my buddy. I hardly know him.]
TREAT: He's a handsome son of a bitch though, isn't he?
[PHILIP: He's handsome, all right.]
TREAT: Did you see the film?
[PHILLIP: Yes.]
TREAT: I bet there's not a goddamn film you haven't seen. I mean, I bet you're a fucking walking encyclopedia of the film in-

dustry.

[PHILLIP: I seen every one of his films.]

TREAT: That's what I'm saying. I'm also wondering what a famous movie star like him is doing hanging around North Philly, sneaking into people's houses, underlining words, underlining sentences, even phrases.

[PHILLIP: I wouldn't know.]

TREAT: Here I am sitting watching Errol Flynn on horseback, leading the famous Charge of the Ten Thousand, when suddenly I hear something. Wadaya think I heard?

[PHILLIP: I don't know, Treat.]

TREAT: I'm watching Errol Flynn on TV and at the same time out of the corner of my eye I see the bastard sneaking around my house. The fucker is a glutton for punishment, Phillip. I mean, the last time he was here he hadda jump out a second story window. He could've broken his neck, could've ruined his career. Hollywood ain't interested in no leading man with a broken neck. What kinda parts is he gonna play . . . broken neck parts! Corpses! Maybe even the Hunchback of Notre Dame! He must have been hanging around here for years, Phillip! Look! *(Pulls out the books from under the couch) Life on the Mississippi,* by Mark Twain! *The Count of fucking Monte Cristo! The Arabian Nights!* Books, books, everywhere and in each of these books, underlined words, thousands of underlined words. And look what else I found! *(Pulls out the red shoe)* Imagine that! All this time we was thinking she was some kind of one-legged tramp when all along she had two legs. She does have an unusual problem though. This is a shoe for a right foot and the shoe we threw out that window was for another right foot, which leads me to believe that this woman has two right feet. What the fuck does she look like, Phillip, some kind of awful monster roaming the Philadelphia streets, leaning to the right. *(*HE *hurls the shoe against the wall.* HE *fixes himself a drink)* I think that's the last of Errol Flynn, though, Phillip.

114

[PHILLIP: Wadaya mean?]

TREAT: I caught him dead to rights. He's not gonna bother us ever again.

[PHILLIP: What did you do?]

TREAT: I cut off his hands. *(Pause)* I had no choice. You didn't happen to see him on the way home, did you?

A PIECE OF MONOLOGUE   Samuel Beckett

Curtain.

Faint diffuse light.

Speaker stands well off center downstage audience left.

White hair, white nightgown, white socks.

Two metres to his left, same level, same height, standard lamp, skull-sized white globe, faintly lit.

Just visible extreme right, same level, white foot of pallet bed.

Ten seconds before speech begins.

Thirty seconds before end of speech lamplight begins to fail.

Lamp out. Silence. Speaker, globe, foot of pallet, barely visible in diffuse light.

Ten seconds.

Curtain.

SPEAKER: Birth was the death of him. Again. Words are few. Dying too. Birth was the death of him. Ghastly grinning ever since. Up at the lid to come. In cradle and crib. At suck first fiasco. With the first totters. From mammy to nanny and back. All the way. Bandied back and forth. So ghastly grinning on. From funeral to funeral. To now. This night. Two and a half billion seconds. Again. Two and a half billion seconds. Hard to believe so few. From funeral to funeral. Funerals of . . . he all but said of loved ones. Thirty thousand nights. Hard to believe so few. Born dead of night. Sun long sunk behind the larches. New needles turning green. In the room dark gaining. Till faint light from standard lamp. Wick turned low. And now. This night. Up at nightfall. Every nightfall. Faint light in room. Whence unknown. None from window. No. Next to none. No such thing as none. Gropes to window and stares out. Stands there staring out. Stock still staring out. Nothing stirring in that black vast. Gropes back in the end to where the lamp is standing. Was standing. When last went out. Loose matches in right-hand pocket. Strikes one on his buttock the way his father taught him. Takes off a milkwhite globe and sets it down. Match goes out. Strikes a second as before. Takes off chimney. Smoke-clouded. Holds it in left hand. Match goes out. Strikes a third as before and sets it to wick. Puts back chimney. Match goes out. Puts back globe. Turns wick low. Backs away to edge of light and turns to face east. Blank wall. So nightly. Up. Socks. Nightgown. Window. Lamp. Backs away to edge of light and stands facing blank wall. Covered with pictures once. Pictures of . . . he all but said of loved ones. Unframed. Unglazed. Pinned to wall with drawing-pins. All shapes and sizes. Down one after another. Gone. Torn to shreds and scattered.

PLENTY   David Hare

Easter 1962. An apartment in Knightsbridge, a well-to-do section of London. RAYMOND BROCK *(40s), the long-suffering and ineffectual diplomat husband of the difficult* SUSAN TRAHERNE, *finally vents* HIS *anger.* HE *is set off when* SUSAN *smashes an expensive ornament.*

BROCK: Your life is selfish, self-interested gain. That's the most charitable interpretation to hand. You claim to be protecting some personal ideal, always at a cost of almost infinite pain to everyone around you. You are selfish, you are brutish, you are unkind. You are jealous of other people's happiness as well, determined to de-

116

stroy other ways of happiness they find. I've spend fifteen years of my life trying to help you, simply trying to be kind, and my great comfort has been that I am waiting for some indication from you . . . some sign that you have valued this kindness of mine. Some love perhaps. Insane. *(HE smiles)* And yet . . . I shan't every really give in, I won't surrender till you're well again. And that to me would mean your admitting one thing: that in the life you have led you have utterly failed, failed in the very, very heart of your life. Admit that. Then perhaps you might really move on. *(Pause)* Now I'm going to go and give our doctor a ring. I plan at last to beat you at your own kind of game. I am going to play as dirtily and ruthlessly as you. And this time I am certainly not giving in. *(BROCK goes out. A pause.)*

PRAVDA   Howard Brenton & David Hare

The present. The Yorkshire moors of England. LAMBERT LE ROUX (40s), heavily built, muscular and dark, is dressed for hunting. LE ROUX is the powerful and sinister owner of a chain of newspapers world-wide. HE is from South Africa. HE laughs and sneers at the attempts of ANDREW MAY to expose HIS criminal past. LE ROUX destroys MAY's will to resist and serves a slander suit on him.

LE ROUX: Control yourself, man.

(LE ROUX moves quietly and picks up the envelope)

I come to this country to organize your lives. I do nothing. People fall before me as if they had been waiting. Why should I lift a gun? People disgrace themselves around me. Sell their property, emigrate, betray their friends, even before I ask them. Give in. "Oh he's not as bad as I expected." From you alone there is a trace of resistance. But you seem to have no idea how to use it, how to destroy. You should hit a man in the face to make his face disappear.

117

In England you can never fight because you do not know what you believe.

(A pause. Then ANDREW *sinks to his knees.* LE ROUX *smiles)*

You are always reading books and disagreeing and arguing, and taking votes. In my house in Weybridge I have a thousand books. But I don't need to read them. Because my mind is made up.

(There is a pause. LE ROUX *seems momentarily lost in thought)*

I had a hotel in Blomfontein. Just three hundred bedrooms or so. And the hotel had a copying machine. On the à la carte menu they did a little drawing, "Chef of the day." Then I found a very witty waiter who wrote things about other hotels. Unkind things. About less good hotels. It became fashionable in Blomfontein to eat in my hotel and read these little comments. Then I thought "Oh people will appreciate this more if they have to pay for it." And the menu turned into the *Blomfontein Vortrekker. (HE smiles again)* I'm still not interested in papers. I like *The Victory's* name. I'm thinking of concessions. Tea-towels, pillow cases, exploitation. That's what I like. *(HE shakes his head.)* Good papers are no good. There's no point in them. All that writing. Why go to the trouble of producing good ones, when bad ones are so much easier? And they sell better too.

[ANDREW: I'm beaten, I know. The landscape is blasted. Every decent hope people had, blasted. I just cling to this idea of the language. That a sentence means something. Hang on to the sentence. "On the one hand, on the ... "]

(HIS voice dies. There are tears in HIS eyes. LE ROUX *squats beside* HIM *and whispers into* HIS *ear like a lover.)*

LE ROUX: Editorial freedom. You never used it when you had it. It is fast gone. Why should you deserve freedom any more?

(HE puts the writ gently in ANDREW's *mouth. The stage darkens. A wind blows across the moor.* LE ROUX *stands and turns towards us. Then* HE *begins to 'ti-tum ti-tum' to himself.)*

LE ROUX: Ti-tum ti-tum ti-tum titti tum ...

A PRELUDE TO DEATH IN VENICE

Lee Breuer

The present. On the street at night. JOHN GREED, *a puppet manipulated by* BILL, *stands at two touch-tone pay phones where* HE/THEY *make a series of telephone calls to different aspects of* JOHN's *life.* BILL's *voice is* JOHN's *voice.* BOTH *are dressed in a similar but not identical way.* JOHN, *in a state of anxiety, receives a callback from "Johns Anonymous," beginning a monologue filled with wordplays and associations that touch on the various "roles"* JOHN *plays.*

JOHN: *(On* PHONE I*)* "Johns Anonymous." Well, look in the commercial listings. It's not in the commercial listings? I just got it from the commercial listings. Well, give me the supervisor. There's no supervisor? Well, give me my dime. What do you mean, "It's not my dime!" *(Hangs up)*

JOHN: *(To* BILL*)* You got another dime?

BILL *shakes his head.*

JOHN: *(To* BILL, *continued)* What do you mean, "You don't got another dime!"

Anxious pause until PHONE I *rings.*

JOHN: *(Answering* PHONE I*)* "Johns Anonymous!" Whew . . . How'd you get my number? Oh . . . you called my Mother. Now she's giving out my number. I was picking up my messages. Sometimes you get long messages. Tom called. "Tom," man. "Tom!" Well, it's not hard to understand—the word is out, "I want to shoot in Venice"; he's pushing a script. Why should I mind? I don't write my scripts. I'm a "shooter" by profession—that's what I profess—I mean, I'm a "straight shooter." My problems lie in the area of projection. I remember, once, projecting "Imitation of Life" onto my dog. I made a mistake; it was a conceptual error. No, the problem was, this small domestic animal projected "Beauty and the Beast" right back on me. I was perceived. I perceived myself per-

119

ceived. Right. I perceived I was not just some "Tom" "Dick" or "Harry." No, I was a "Jean." Right. I perceived that I, myself, was not a self-supporting system. I was a reactive system. I followed the action—all I needed was a little action. I followed other dogs; I panned around looking for little pussy cats; I zoomed in on a gerbil once because she thought I looked like Steve McQueen. Then I realized that my shooting was affected. I discovered that my shooting was affected shooting a long shot on Twenty-Third Street. Formerly, when shooting, light entered my aperture, through my lens, and left an image right between my sprocket holes. But, now, my light goes through my lens the other way and leaves my image on Twenty-Third Street. This was detailed in an article by Annette Michaelson called "The Greed Effect"—that's how it's referred to in the Industry today; in other circles it's called "The Miracle of Twenty-Third Street"—it depends on your circle. Well, frankly, I had a creative crisis—three shots a day, then two, for a while there I was down to eighteen frames a week on Sunday afternoons. Then I cut out color. There I was down to black and white. I'd wake up in the morning with the shakes, my hair came out. I went on a bender; I shot two reels of "Todd AO" with quadrophonic sound. Afterwards, I was hospitalized. I emerged from the hospital a changed John. I was a "Mark." "You're a junkie, John," they told me, "you've got to go cold cock." I said, "I can't do it, Doc. I've found myself. I'm hooked on my reality. Now, I'm afraid to fade. My self is my vacation." What can I do? I go into myself. I become self involved. I try to be self effacing. But, that's self defeating. I indulge in self recrimination. But all that does is make me more self centered. I long to be self trancending. But, this becomes too self deluding, which brings me to the brink of self destruction, which becomes a subject of self concern. Am I being self indulgent? Good. Good. Just checking. You got to help me, man, I'm going down the garden path—self assertion, then, self direction, then I get just plain old selfish—after which followeth self possession. I'm beside myself. That's the Pale Horse, man. I'm on the edge. I'm on the edge of being a "self made," man.

THE PROFESSIONAL FRENCHMAN
John Wellman

The present during a raging snowstorm. A home in suburban Virginia just outside Washington, D.C. It is Thanksgiving Day. SAM (30s-40s), an enterprising American businessman of questionable background and avid football fan, has just lost a bet on the Oakland Raiders-Cleveland Browns game to JACQUES, a "professional Frenchman." SAM offers this strange and sardonic advice to one of the guests of the house, the Belgian woman MEVROUW.

SAM: Take my advice, *Mevrouw.* Never
Gamble against professionals.
They are merciless.
(They laugh. Pause. SAM speaks in a strange, demoniacal, deep voice)
You have to beat them into submission. Once
You get a man down
In America, blessèd America,
You have to fucking pound
Him into the clay, you have
To finish him off. Destroy
Him. Pulverize him. Be-
Cause if you show a man
Any mercy. Any kindness.
If you leave him with any
Small part of his self-respect
He'll never forgive you, he'll
Make you bloody well pay

121

For every fucking thing you
Ever did. For him.
    Never give a man a second chance.
When you get the opportunity
To eat a human being
Swallow him whole
Or grind him to
Pulp, but never NEVER
Leave the tiniest bit
Of living humanity left
Or you'll be sorry for it.
    You can bet your ass
Reagan won't. Reagan-Reagan
The First. Year One of Reagan-
Reagan. Just like Bokassa.
A perfectly honed human machine.
Only Bokassa was too mild.
He didn't eat up all the children.
He left some. We had it all,
    Rusty, we had it all.
We fine-spirited humanitarian people.
But we succumbed to our sense of
Mercy. We had the Nixons of
The world beaten and begging.
And we took pity and gave them
Mercy. It's going to snow a
Hundred years and Reagan
Will have no mercy, you can
Be sure of that. We'll all be
Buried so deep in the ice-box
Of history no one will ever
Know we existed. Never.

THE REAL THING   Tom Stoppard

The present. A London living room/study. HENRY *(40-ish), a
successful writer and wit, has been jealously arguing with* ANNIE
over a convict and would-be writer named BRODIE. ANNIE *begins to get the advantage over* HENRY *and, in exasperation,* HE
tries to explain to HER *the essence of good writing.* HENRY *uses a
cricket bat to illustrate* HIS *point.*

HENRY: Jesus, Annie, you're beginning to appal me. There's
something scary about stupidity made coherent. I can deal with id-
iots, and I can deal with sensible argument, but I don't know how to
deal with you. Where's my cricket bat?[. . .]No, I'm serious.
(HE goes out while she watches in wary disbelief. HE *returns with
an old cricket bat)* Right, you silly cow—
[ANNIE: Don't you bloody dare—]
HENRY: Shut up and listen. This thing here, which looks like a
wooden club, is actually several pieces of particular wood cunningly
put together in a certain way so that the whole thing is sprung, like a
dance floor. It's for hitting cricket balls with. If you get it right, the
cricket ball will travel two hundred yards in four seconds, and all
you've done is give it a knock like knocking the top off a bottle of
stout, and it makes a noise like a trout taking a fly . . . *(HE clucks
his tongue to make the noise)* What we're trying to do is to write
cricket bats, so that when we throw up an idea and give it a little
knock, it might . . . *travel* . . . *(HE clucks his tongue again and
picks up the script)* Now, what we've got here is a lump of wood of
roughly the same shape trying to be a cricket bat, and if you hit a
ball with it, the ball will travel about ten feet and you will drop the
bat and dance about shouting "Ouch!" with your hands stuck into
your armpits. *(Indicating the cricket bat)* This isn't better because
someone says it's better, or because there's a conspiracy by the
MCC to keep cudgels off the field. It's better because it's better.
You don't believe me, so I suggest you go out to bat with this and

123

see how you get on. "You're a strange boy, Billy, how old are you?" "Twenty, but I've lived more than you'll ever live." Ooh, ouch!

(HE *drops the script and hops about with his hands in his armpits, going "Ouch!"* ANNIE *watches him expressionlessly until* HE *desists.*)

THE RESURRECTION OF LADY LESTER
OyamO

1930s. A seedy New York hotel room overlooking the jazz club "Birdland." LESTER YOUNG *(40s), the legendary jazz musician, is sickly, coughing, and nearing* HIS *death.* HE *opens the play with this monologue, partly sung and party recited. In the second monologue, a flashback to a car on the road, traveling between gigs, one of* LESTER YOUNG's *side musicians,* LINCOLN, *talks about* HIS *past and the life of poverty* HE *escaped.*

LESTER: UM JUST A DRIED-UP CORN COB
SINGING IN THE SWEET HOT SUN
UM JUST A DRIED-UP CORN COB . . . *(Talking)* What's wrong? You don't think I can sing? I can carry a melody at least and when I drop this lip extension *(Indicating* HIS *horn)* in my chops, I blow soft little stories that make you cry they sound so true.
(Singing again but with musical accompaniment.)
LESTER: UM JUST A DRIED-UP CORN COB
DUSTY IN THE SWEET HOT SUN
UM JUST A DRIED-UP CORN COB
DUSTY IN THE SWEET HOT SUN
MY BLOOD IS FLYIN' AWAY
I GUESS MY TRIP IS ALMOST DONE

(Talking blues. Stop time.)
LESTER: I HAD ALL THE WOMEN
DRANK DOWN ALL THE WINE
BLUE UP ALL THE NOTES
RAN A MILLION STOP SIGNS
(Talking again, with music under.)
How yaw feelin'?
How yaw feelin' peekin' at a phony ghost?
The Prez, Mr. Lester Young, President—
I was president when presidents were good men and bop was in—
I know yaw out there listening;
I may be sick, crazy, talk to myself, drink gin like a dog, and black,
But I ain't no communist;
I'm just yo' typical, innocent unamerican—*(Pointing to his head)*
Everybody I want to say anything to is right here, you dig?
They can't be no other place now,
But somebody up here know something,
Something that I have to know now.
I have been resurrected from the Land of the True Living Harmony
Where God sings in everybody's soul
And we all got it made—
I came here in the first beat to live,
You dig?
I came to hear a vision of simple love,
Fresh love, you dig?
I wanted to serve the Music
And smile bravely in its light
Because I had to—
I had to feel my way in the music—
I was a dumb child
And the music led me to secrets
Hidden in my own heart,
Secrets about what really matters

125

When you know you're a human person
And not a human monkey.
I came here to jam with my fellow sounds,
To help weave a cloth of light, soft harmony,
So my family,
None of you,
Don't have to be naked
In this drafty-ass world of the intelligent beast—
But there was something I didn't see—
There was something I never found—

* * *

LINCOLN: Check this out: My daddy was dead for ten years before he finally died from a serious lack of money. In Georgia, a sharecropper with nine crummies in a two room shack. Daddy didn't drink his miseries away 'cause he couldn't afford to drink. He used to come home all bent over every evening, wash up, eat some corn meal mush or grits with fatback bacon or collards and okra with fatback or fatback with turnips and cornbread. That's why I don't eat no pork. Then, after he'd eat and maybe grunt at his family, he'd take his raggedy harmonica and go sit under a tree just down the road from the shack, and he'd watch the road and the cotton fields and play the meanest blues I ever heard until it was time for him to go to bed. He did that every day, all year, year in and year out, good weather and bad. Hardly ever spoke a word. He started wasting away from the inside, and, even if we could have afforded to call a doctor, I don't think it would have done any good. Money, honey. When he died, I got on that same road he used to dream about and I ain't never looked back to Georgia or poverty ever since. I didn't make the laws of this land, but the law says that money keeps you alive, well and looking good. That's the secret of why I stay so pretty.

RIVKALA'S RING   Spalding Gray

This a Chekhov short story adapted by the writer/performer
SPALDING GRAY. HIS *first-person narrative about the creation*
of the piece, and details from HIS *own life, form the basis of the*
monologue.

THE PERSON: The day the Chekhov short story arrived I saw
my first missing child. On a milk carton. And found a drowned rat
in our pool. The photo of the child barely left an impression; it was
like any black-and-white photograph of any child anywhere. The
more I studied the face, the more it broke up and blended into ab-
stract dots; and besides, I hadn't seen any stray children in the
neighborhood. I hadn't seen any children. For that matter, I hadn't
seen any people either. There were plenty of houses, but no people.
Renée and I were subletting in the Hollywood Hills just below the
Hollywood sign. And all the Venetian blinds in all the houses were
always closed. And everyone seemed deep dark inside, writing final drafts of their latest TV scripts. Our swimming pool was bigger
than our apartment. And much colder. It wasn't heated and we
could only look at it and never go in.

Anyway, the particular morning the Chekhov short story arrived,
I was on my way to fetch the mail when I noticed the drowned rat
floating in among the eucalyptus leaves. The wind had blown wild
the night before. A mighty Santa Ana had swept in under a full
moon, turning everything upside down. Electricity was blown out
and semitrailers were overturned in the lowlands. I couldn't sleep.
The wind came in and stirred me and reminded me so much, too
much, of raw indifferent nature. The bare-boned breath of the
desert whipping in over this crazy glitter town.

So maybe the rat had blown out of the palm tree. Joe, our
upstairs neighbor, said that the rats lived in palm trees and that they
often drowned in the pool because they were too stupid to use the
steps. Or more like their little feet didn't go down that deep. Joe
said that when the weather got real hot, all the various creatures
came down early out of the Hollywood Hills to take a dip in the

pool: coyote, raccoons, and skunks—all sorts of stuff. And they had the good sense to use the steps of the pool, swim a few measured laps, and then jog back into the hills where they belonged. I pictured a possum in little Nike jogging shoes shaking off the water from his fur and jogging off toward the Hollywood sign.

But I couldn't help calling Renée's attention to this drowned rat—the way it hung there so suspended in the pool with his little legs dangling and his white whiskers out, fully suspended in the water—like it was still alive, or stuffed. Like Mr. Rat, you know, like Mr. Comic Book Rat. Mr. Unharmful Stuffed Rat. The way the water held those whiskers out made me call out to Renée: "Renée! Come quick, come quickly, you've got to see this!"

And she, having no idea what I was talking about, scurried out like a little kid. Scurried out barefoot with her hands clasped across her chest like this little excited kid. And then when she saw what it was, she started screaming and said, "Get it out! Get the net. Get it out!" She couldn't look at it.

It wasn't that I was trying to torture Renée. It was more like a piece of me was missing; the screaming part was missing. Like Renée always said, "I love you but you're a funny guy because you have a piece of your pie missing. Sometimes you don't react in a normal human way to stuff that needs a scream or a cry." And then she does it for me. So Renée completes me, you see. She makes up for the missing piece of the pie. I needed her to be upset about the rat. Then and only then could I toss that sad swollen rat body into the rotten palm leaves and have done with it.

There was another rat, come to think of it. There was another rat in our life in New York City just before we moved to Hollywood. But first, let me tell you what was happening out here just before the Chekhov story came.

128

ROAD   Jim Cartwright

*The present. A dilapidated row of houses in a depressed city of
Northern England. An out-of-work young man, JOEY (20s), is
sitting up in bed with HIS arm around HIS girlfriend, CLARE. She
sleeps. JOEY has been starving himself to death in a kind of personal protest. Weak with strain, HE speaks out.*

JOEY: I feel like England's forcing the brain out me head. I'm
sick of it. Sick of it all. People reading newspapers: "EURO-
VISION LOVERS", "OUR QUEEEN MUM," "MAGGIE'S
TEARS", being fooled again and again. What the fuck-fuck is it?
Where am I? Bin lying here two weeks now. On and on through
the strain. I wear pain like a hat. Everyone's insane. The world
really is a bucket of devil sick. Every little moment's stupid. I'm
sick of people-people, stupid people. Frying the air with their
mucky words, their mucky thoughts, their mucky deeds. Horrible
sex being had under rotten bedding. Sickly sex being had on the
waterbed. Where has man gone? Why is he so wrong? Why am I
hurt all through? Every piece of me is bruised or gnawed raw, if
you could see it, my heart's like an elbow. I've been done through
by them, it, the crushing sky of ignorance, thigh of pignorance.
What did I do! What was my crime? Who do I blame? God for
giving me a spark of vision? Not enough of one, not enough of the
other, just enough for discontent, enough to have me right out on
the edge. Not able to get anyone out here with me, not able to get in
with the rest. Oh God I'm so far gone it's too late. I'm half dead
and I'm not sad or glad. I'm not sad or glad, what a fucking,
bastard, bitching, cunt state to be in. I'm black inside. Bitterness
has swelled like a mighty black rose inside me. Its petals are
creaking against my chest. I want it out! out! out! Devil, God,
Devil, God, Devil, God, save me something. Anything. There's
got to be summat will come to help us. If only we can make the
right state. If I can only get myself into the right state. This is it.

This is why I'm on the diet. *(HE looks around, remembering)* Fucking hell am I in a film or what? Or snot, or what. *(HE is tightening)* Plans wilted like weak plants, stems too long too soon. They put their thumbs on our heads, but I resisted and cracked my skull. What a silly thing to go and do, Joey. I cracked my spirit against a 25,000 ton marshmallow called them, them, them. Them who hold the power in their dry hands. the problem-makers and solvers all in. IIIIIIIIIIIII bring up small white birds covered in bile and fat blood, they was my hopes. I bring up a small hard pig that was my destiny. I'd like to bring it all out but bbbbbbbbbbbut I've gone all constipated on bitterness, it won't remove itself. God give me a laxative if you got one. Ha! AArrrrrgh! Arrrrgh! Oh AAArrrrrgh! *(HE's sweating and straining)* Come out, come out, you tight bastard. Oh no! Death suck me up through that straw inside my spine! No leave me! Oh I'm full of dark frost. Who's done this to me! And why? Oh why? Is it worth that extra bit of business to see me suffer, is it? I blame you BUSINESS and you RELIGION its favourite friend, hand in hand YOU HAVE MURDERED THE CHILD IN MAN! MURDERERS! CUNTS! I'D LIKE TO CUT OPEN YOUR BELLIES AND SEE THE BROWN POUR!

(It should appear that HE's going to get out of bed to really kill somebody. Then CLARE wakes. SHE puts HER arm on HIM.)

SAFE SEX   Harvey Fierstein

A stage. GHEE and MEAD are two gay lovers having an argument while trying to keep their balance on a huge, theatrical see-saw. They are dressed in night shirts. GHEE ponders the question of love and how AIDS has corrupted it.

GHEE: You know that you were my first love. My only love. Except if you count you then and you now. But then you'd have to

130

count me then and me now so I guess "Only" still goes.

I was a baby. You were all growed up.

I practically lost my virginity. You'd practically lost count.

I tiptoed through your life, living on the edges, covering my tracks, remaining secret and quiet and was quite happy.

They were different times.

(Considers)

Is it enough to say that they were different times? You had a life, I had a life and we had a life.

You lived in your world, and I had my world and then we shared a bed.

We had great sex, but argued politics: To be or not to be in the closet, separatism, legalization, legislation . . .

Politics were argued, sex was great.

Different times.

I believe that there were fewer Nautilus machines then. There were certainly fewer gyms. We were certainly happier with ourselves. And we loved each other.

We shared what we could when we could and our anger was for them that would not let us be. Our fear was of them that would not let us be. Our comfort was being with each other.

Not so different. But different enough.

When I picture you then I see a man prone on my bed and waiting. No expectations or demands. Just a man waiting to be with another man where he was happy and belonged. A nervous smile, an unassumed pose, patient, excited, warm and delicious.

(Happy pause)

We were together without questing. We were there, at that moment, in the present, together. Perfectly balanced; need and satisfaction. Evenly matched. We soared.

And sex, like air and water, was unimportant.

We had no lists of "Do's and Don't's", there was no death count. The worst you could get from loving was a broken heart. Which you gave me. And I lived. Remember crabs? Remember worrying about clap? Remember herpes?

Different times.

And we were invisible. No one knew who we were for real. Ignored by the press, taunted by politicians, envied for our freedom by the young who were not us. We were the great chic mysterious underground and I loved every minute.

And then came now.

Different times.

Now we enjoy politics and argue sex.

(Laughs)

Now we're indistinguishable. Now we've been defined by them. Now they know that we're the same.

We're counted in their surveys, we're numbered in their watchfulness, we're powered in their press. We're courted, polled, placated . . . Now they know who we are. The myths slowly peel away and the mysteries fade. Now they see that we're doctors and lawyers and priest and teachers and mothers and babies. Now they see us everywhere; hospitals, classrooms, theatres, obituaries . . .

"Joe Doe. Age twenty-seven. Cause of death—AIDS related pnuemonia. Survived by Mother, Father, Sister, Brother, Dog, Cat, Fish and friend." Now when they tell lies about us we can answer. We have found our voices. They know who we are. They know we care what they think. And all because of a disease. A virus. A virus that you get, not because you're gay, but because you're human.

(Looks down at MEAD *desperately)*

If anyone tried to tell me that one day I'd push you to the other side of the bed . . . ?

(Laughs)

But I did. I did because it wasn't safe to love anyone as much as I loved you. And that was then.

Now? I love you more right now than I did on our most carefree day. I trust you more than before you renounced our commitment. I need you more now than I did when you were away from me. I want you more now ... And it's impossible. Even if you fought me and won. Even if you broke through and got me to admit who you truly are to me ... We can never touch as before. We can never be as before. "Now" will always define us.

Different times. Too late.

At last we have "Safe Sex." Safe for them.

THE SEX ORGAN   John Quincy Long

The present. Offices of an advertising agency. TED is trying to free associate HIS way towards a new "concept" that will sell a product. HIS monologue is a trip through that process.

TED: Okay
Okay
What's the product?

[HELEN: Budweiser]

TED: Budweiser
Budweiser
Budweiser Beer
Good beer
Terrific beer
Beer's beer
Drinker's beer
Drink drink
Drunk drink
Drink of drinks
Drink of drunks

Kinky drink
Gamey drink
The game drink
Drink at the game
Drink with the boys at the game
Game
Game
Sport
The drink of sports
Sporting life
Boy's life
Life in prison
Homicide
Murder
Murder plot
Abattoire
Abbot
Abbott
and Costello?
No
Abbot
Abbot
About
A boot
Das Boot
Boot!
Couldn't pour piss out of a boot

That's it
Fishing
The guys
Fishing
Hip boots
You know

134

Waders
Big rubber boots
Our guy is showing the other guys his waders
New waders his wife just bought him
Flexing suspenders
Tromping around
Into the river at last
Sighs of pleasure
Whoops
There's a leak
No there isn't
The guys
The buddies
They've snuck up and filled his waders with water
With a hose
With a bucket full of minnows
No
I got it
I got it
The guy
Our guy
He gets these boots as a Christmas present
Right?
From his son daughter wife mother father grandfather
Whatever
Shots of the family under the tree
Shots of whoever handing Dad his lumpengift
What could it be?
Surprise
Waders
Cute
He fantasizes himself to the river with his buddies
Budweiser in hand

No
No
Better yet
Much better
He's cleaning out . . .
The other's too complicated
He's cleaning out the closet
No
The garage
Yeah
The garage
Cleaning out the garage by himself
Oh tedium
What a drag
Finds the waders
By himself in the garage he finds the waders
He puts them on feeling deliciously silly
Fantasy
Fantasy
He's at the river
He can almost see it
We can almost see it
Maybe we do see it
I don't know
He's casting
The trout are nibbling
MacNibbles?
No
Then
His buddies are there
Horsing around
À la loo
À la loo

Fun fun fun
Drink drink drink
Then sonofabitch
His buddies are there
They really are
Peeking in through the dirty garage window
Watching him
Laughing
Friends
Friendly friends
Looking through the window
Sweatshirts
Baseball caps askew
Then
Payoff
They hold up . . .

[HELEN: The beer]

TED: The Bud
Ho
God
Whatafuckinconcept

SLAM!   **Jane Willis**

*The present. A dank, dirty, dark men's room in a punk club on
New York's lower East Side. It is a Tuesday night during the
band's set-break. MEL (19ish), a high school student from Flush-
ing, Queens, is having a brooding and confusing conversation with
HIS older friend LINCOLN. BOTH are in punk dress and are avid
"slam dancers."*

MEL: I know exactly what you mean.

[LINC: Yeah?]

MEL: It's goin' through the motions. You wake up, have a relationship with somebody. Hello Goodbye—it's over before it began.

[LINC: Slam bam.]

MEL: Thank you ma'am. You eat. Listen to other people talk. Pop some brown-haired, grey-eyed chick on Saturday night. Make a point of askin' her her name. Maybe write down her phone number . . . and you look at yourself a year later and all you've got are a bunch of dirty little slips of paper in your coat pocket. A goddamn atlas of pencil-scratched phone numbers. What could of been. But you forgot to write the fuckin' names down above the numbers! And not only that, but you look around you and it seems like EVERYBODY you know is slippin' away from you and suddenly you've got nobody to reflect you, good or bad on the outside an' inside. You're slippin away from yourself because you just can't keep up! You can't keep up! You honestly can't remember what you said you wanted to be when you grew up. *(Stabs his knife in the stall)* But you can't go around bein' hurt and confused all the time, so you lock yourself up a little bit—til you start to feel like somethin' outta the *Invasion of the Body Snatchers*. The only time you get to release is here—when you and a bunch of other guys can knock themselves numb. MAKE IT ALL GO AWAY. The thing I love about this place isn't the music—or ramming head or throwin' myself off the stage—the thing I love here is knowing that everybody else came here for the same reason as me. TO GET OUT OF THEMSELVES! It makes me feel . . . close. But, as for tomorrow, and the rest of the week, I'll go back to being a robot. A zombie. A clone. I feel the exact same way you do, Linc. Like a Droid.

SWIMMING TO CAMBODIA   Spalding Gray

This selection is from a book of monologues written and performed by SPALDING GRAY *about events surrounding* HIS *work in the film,* THE KILLING FIELDS. *Here* HE *tells a story, tinged with some envy, about one of the stars of that film.*

It was time for dinner and a bunch of us went to an outdoor restaurant right on the edge of the Indian Ocean. There were about twenty of us and it all looked and felt like a big Thanksgiving dinner, the Last Supper right at the edge of the world. The islands beyond, over which sweet, cooling trade winds blew, gave off no light or life. It was just us and the Thai waiters moving under multicolored Japanese lanterns that swayed in the winds.

David Puttnam sat at the head of the table and I sat to his left with my back to the sea. David was holding up a picture of John Malkovich and saying, "So, I hear John doesn't want to do any more films. He says he wants to return to the Steppenwolf Theatre Company in Chicago." John was sitting at the far end of the table and I was a little drunk and saying, "Yes, I think the lady doth protheth too much." John was winking back at me and taking it all good-naturedly.

Now, I was feeling a little competitive, I admit it. I had been doing solo performance for so long that I had forgotten all that competitive stuff that comes up when you begin to mix and mingle with a lot of Talent. I had been down at the Performing Garage for so long that I'd lost touch with that scene. I know that not only is John a good actor, he's also a good storyteller. He could be sitting behind a table just like I do somewhere far away, let's say in Chicago or Alaska, telling stories not unlike these.

My question is, could I play Biff on Broadway? Are we interchangeable? John just gets work. It seems to just come to him because he's not needy. Also, he has a good manager. It's not just that he has an agent, he also has a *very good* manager. In fact, I don't know if you noticed, but when *The Killing Fields* was reviewed in *The New York Times,* there was also a small article in another part of the paper about the blackout on the Q.E. II, and who did they contact to interview by telephone satellite? John Malkovich. How did he get on the Q.E. II? His manager. And how did *The Times* know he was there? His manager. And how did the lights go out? (And how did Ronald Reagan become President?) They set it up like that to get the reverb. It's an echo—you see, the review isn't enough.

TALLEY AND SON   Lanford Wilson

July 4, 1944. The TALLEY *home outside Lebanon, Missouri.* TIMMY TALLEY *(20), killed in the Pacific during the Second World War, speaks to the audience throughout the play as a ghostly commentator. Here* HE *tells about falling in battle.*

TIMMY: Dad said he didn't even know where I fell. That official "fell." Like a lotta people he gets very—not just correct, but formal—under pressure. Hell, "fell" isn't the half of it. Splatted is more like it. Didn't feel a thing. Shock and whatnot takes care of that. I felt a force all against me and suddenly I've got a different angle on the terrain. I'm looking up into the trees instead of out across the jungle floor. I thought, How am I looking at that? Then I thought, Oh, sure, I'm flat on my ass looking up. Some squawking parrot up there looking down at me; gonna drop it right on my face. I figgered, all right, this part is easy. I just lay here till some corpsman comes up and does his job. You get very philosophical. Then the corpsmen come and, oh, Daddy, I knew from the look on their faces that this is bad. This young recruit, couldn't be sixteen, turned around and I thought he was gonna puke, but he flat out fainted before he had the chance. You could tell he'd enlisted in this thing ten minutes after seeing *To the Shores* *of Tripoli.* Then all of a sudden I'm on a stretcher and they're rushing me off to somewhere. You understand, you don't feel the stretcher under you, you just know they're rushing you to somewhere. You're looking up into the sun; some guy is running along beside you, trying to keep his hand over your eyes, shade them from the sun; you'd kinda rather see it. And all the corpsmen are still looking so cut-up I said, "Hey, do you raggedy-asses think I don't know you're razzing me? I got a pass to go home, you're trying to make me think I won't get there." Or, actually, I thought I said that; then I realized nothing had come out. I thought, Well, hell, if this isn't a lousy predicament. You always wondered if it comes will you fall all to pieces, and now it's come and I'm doing fine and damned proud of it and nobody is gonna know. *(TALLY enters from the kitchen and exits out the front door)* Granddad Talley would say, "Pride goeth before a fall, sir." Should have known it. Of course, you do know that the body is doing what the body does. You can feel—barely, a little bit—that your body is urinating all over itself and your bowels are letting go something fierce. You try to get ahold with your mind of the muscles down in your belly that you use to hold it off, but your mind can't find em. *(Pause)* If those guys hadn't looked so bad, you might have gone all to pieces, but they're so torn up, you feel somebody has got to take this thing lightly.

TRACERS   John DiFusco

Vietnam War, somewhere out in the field on patrol. A group of soldiers, in formation, move about the stage in slow, cat-like fashion. DINKY DAU (19-20) has this soliloquy.

DINKY DAU: I remember the sky was overcast. It was hot and muggy. Everyone's fatigues were drenched with sweat. It was late afternoon and we hadn't seen shit all day. I don't know what the hell I was thinking about right then, I guess my mind was just sorta blank at that point. I was so damn worn out—we all were. We'd been humpin' all day. My whole body as achin', I could hardly concentrate on the trail in front of me. The jungle on both sides of us started to get real dense, and the trail started goin' downhill. Then all of a sudden, out of nowhere, there were twelve or maybe thirteen VC, right in front of us. *(SCOOTER suddenly freezes, points ahead. The others crouch down)* If the point man hadn't spotted them, they'd have walked right into us. I watched the point man as he raised his weapon. It was like a movie in slow motion. The point man opened up on the first two or three VC. *(SCOOTER opens fire. Music up with gunfire sound effects. The others open fire. All motions are slow and dreamlike)* I watched the first two or three VC go down, and then I opened up on full automatic. I creamed one 'em with an entire clip. I watched my bullets as they ripped across his torso. Everybody was up. Everybody was hyper. Everybody was hittin'. *(HE fumbles with his magazine)* Damn, I wasn't used to reloading. I couldn't get my clip in. Finally I got it. [. . .] Everyone was into it. I was eager. I was angry! [. . .] It was the first time I killed anybody. There were eight or nine dead bodies lying on the ground, and I just kept blasting away at 'em. I just kept blasting away at 'em. [. . .] *(DINKY DAU stares at the bodies. The others begin sweeping the area)* [. . .] It was our little victory. Everybody really got off on that fact. Even the new guy, Baby San, who had a bad case of the combat shakes. [. . .] It was our little victory! [. . .] Eight or nine of the little motherfuckers and not one of us even got a scratch. [. . .] You're dead, motherfucker!

London. Time and place are not specifically stated. The play is an allegory of tough city gangs and late-night club life. MIKE (20s-30s) is the "hero" of the play and a man from North London. HE leads HIS own gang against the Hoxton Mob. Like all characters in the play, MIKE speaks a kind of street poetry that telegraphs moods, actions and sensations. Here HE takes HIS "bird" SYLV out onto the dance floor.

(The CHORUS is seated as in a dance hall. MIKE takes SYLV into the center of the floor. Gradually the others dance around them, holding invisible partners.)

MIKE: Do you wanna dance/I took her on the floor/the crystal ball smashed the light into a million pieces/a shattered lake at sunrise/the music welled up/and the lead guitarist/plugged into ten thousand watts zonging in our ears/callused thumb whipping chords/down the floor we skate/I push her thigh with mine/and backwards she goes to the gentle signal/no horse moved better/and I move my left leg which for a second leaves me hanging on her thigh/then she moves hers/swish/then she's hanging on mine/like I am striding through the sea/our thighs clashing and slicing past each other like huge cathedral bells/whispering past flesh-encased nylon/feeling/all the time knees/pelvis/stomach/hands/fingertips/grip smell/moving interlocking fingers/ice floes melting/skin silk weft and warp/blood-red lips gleaming/pouting/stretching over her hard sharp and wicked-looking Hampsteads/words dripping out her red mouth gush like honey/I lap it up/odors rising from the planet of the flesh/gardens after light showers/hawthorn and wild mimosa/Woolie's best/crushed fag ends/lipstick/powder/gin and tonic/all swarming together on one heavenly nerve-numbing swill/meanwhile huge mountains of aching fleshy worlds are drifting past each other holding their moons/colliding and drifting apart again/the light stings/the journey is over/the guitarist splattered in acne as the rude knife of light stabs him crushes his final shattering chord/the ball of fire stops/and I say thank you very much.

WHEN I WAS A GIRL I USED TO SCREAM AND SHOUT . . . Sharman Macdonald

1966. A rocky beach on the east coast of Scotland. EWAN (16), has come back from swimming and settles down onto the hot rocks. FIONA (16) creeps up on HIM and drops a handful of cold water over HIM.

EWAN: *(Screams)* Fucking cunt.

(FIONA moves away from him and sits staring out to sea. EWAN dries himself meticulously)

Jesus Christ, woman. What do you expect, creeping up on a man like that? Took my breath away. I mean, Jesus, Fiona. That water's freezing. It's not the bloody Mediterranean. What the hell do you have to play bloody stupid games for? I mean, shit, Fiona. Come on. What's a man supposed to do? I mean, shit, Fiona. Shit.

(Pause)

Come here. Look at the bloody face on it. Come here. I forgive you. Come on, I'll give you a cuddle. Bloody hell, woman. Bloody listen, will you. Move your backside over here. I've said I forgive you. Jesus Christ, what do you fucking well want? Dear God, woman, it's not as if I sodding well hit you. I mean, if I'd hit you you'd have something to bloody girn about. Don't be bloody ridiculous.

(Pause)

You want me to say sorry to you. You sodding well do. You do. I sodding well won't. You've not a pissing hope. Shit.

(Pause)

I'm fucking sorry. There. Is that bloody better?

(FIONA moves over to him)

Bloody smile then.

PLAY SOURCES

Beckett, Samuel. *A Piece of Monologue*. In *Rockaby and Other Short Pieces*. New York: Grove Press, 1981.

Berkoff, Steven. *West*. New York: Grove Press, 1985.

Bogosian, Eric. *Funhouse*. In *Drinking in America*. New York: Random House, 1987.

Breuer, Lee. *A Prelude to Death in Venice*. In *Sister Suzie Cinema*. New York: Theatre Communications Group, 1987.

Brenton, Howard and David Hare. *Pravda*. London and New York: Methuen, 1985.

Browne, Stuart. *Dancing Bears*. C/o The Author's Agent, Mary Harden, Bret Adams Ltd., 448 West 44 Street, New York, NY 10036.

Cartwright, Jim. *Road*. London: Methuen, 1986.

Churchill, Caryl. *Cloud Nine*. London and New York: Methuen, 1985.

Cone, Tom. *Herringbone*. In *Plays from Playwright's Horizon*. New York: Broadway Play Publishing. 1987.

Darke, Nick. *The Body*. London: Methuen, 1983.

DiFusco, John, and Vincent Caristi, Richard Chaves, Eric E. Emerson, Rick Gallavan, Merlin Marston, Harry Stephens, and Sheldon Lettich. *Tracers*. New York: Hill & Wang, 1986.

Durang, Christopher. *The Marriage of Bette and Boo*. New York: Grove Press, 1987.

Edgar, David. *The Jail Diary of Albie Sachs*. London: Rex Collings, 1982.

Fierstein, Harvey. *Safe Sex*. C/o The Author's Agent, George Lane, William Morris Agency, 1350 Avenue of the Americas, New York, NY 10019.

Glowacki, Janusz. *Hunting Cockroaches*. In *American Theatre,* May 1987, and *Formations Magazine,* Winter 1986-87, Vol. 3, No. 3.

Gray, Spalding. *Rivkala's Ring*. In *Orchards: Stories by Anton Chekhov and Seven Plays They Have Inspired*. New York: Alfred A. Knopf, 1986.

_____. *Swimming to Cambodia*. New York: Theatre Communications Group, 1986.

Guare, John. *Lydie Breeze*. New York: Dramatists Play Service, 1982.

_____. *Marco Polo Sings a Solo*. New York: Dramatists Play Service, 1977.

Hampton, Christopher. *Les Liasons Dangereuses.* London and Boston: Faber and Faber, 1986.

Hare, David. *Plenty.* New York: Penguin, 1978.

Harwood, Ronald. *The Dresser.* New York: Grove Press, 1980.

Hoffman, William M. *As Is.* New York: Random House, 1985.

Hwang, David Henry. *FOB.* In *New Plays USA 1.* New York: Theatre Communications Group, 1982.

Jenkin, Len. *Five of Us.* New York: Dramatists Play Service, 1986.

Kessler, Lyle. *Orphans.* New York: Samuel French, 1985.

Kopit, Arthur. *The End of the World.* New York: Hill & Wang, 1987.

Kramer, Larry. *The Normal Heart.* New York: New American Library, 1985.

Kureishi, Hanif. *Borderline.* London: Methuen, 1981.

Lauro, Shirley. *Open Admissions.* New York: Samuel French, 1984.

Long, John Quincy. *The Sex Organ.* C/o The Author's Agent, Helen Merrill, 361 West 17 Street, New York, NY 10011.

Macdonald, Sharman. *When I Was a Girl I Used to Scream and Shout . . . .* London: Faber and Faber, 1985.

Mamet, David. *Glengarry Glen Ross.* New York: Grove Press, 1984.

McNally, Terrence. *It's Only a Play.* New York: Dramatists Play Service, 1986.

Medoff, Mark. *Children of a Lesser God.* Salt Lake City, UT: Peregrine Smith Books, 1987.

Metcalfe, Stephen. *The Incredibly Famous Willy Rivers.* In *New Plays USA 3.* New York: Theatre Communications Group, 1986.

Miller, Arthur. *The American Clock.* New York: Dramatists Play Service, 1982.

Mtwa, Percy. *Bopha!* In *Woza Afrika!* New York: George Braziller, 1986.

Ngema, Mbongeni. *Asinamali!* In *Woza Afrika!* New York: George Braziller, 1986.

O'Keefe, John. *Aztec.* In *West Coast Plays 19/20.* Los Angeles: California Theatre Council, 1986.

Overmyer, Eric. *Native Speech.* New York: Broadway Play Publishing, 1984.

OyamO. *The Resurrection of Lady Lester.* In *New Plays USA 1.* New York: Theatre Communications Group, 1982.

Pinter, Harold. *One for the Road*. London: Methuen, 1985.

Pomerance, Bernard. *The Elephant Man*. New York: Grove Press, 1979.

Rabe, David. *Hurlyburly*. New York: Grove Press, 1985.

Rimmer, David. *Album*. New York: Dramatists Play Service, 1981.

Saunders, James. *Bodies*. New York: Dramatists Play Service, 1979.

Shaffer, Peter. *Amadeus*. New York: Samuel French, 1981.

Shanley, John Patrick. *Danny and the Deep Blue Sea*. New York: Dramatists Play Service, 1984.

Shawn, Wallace and André Gregory. *My Dinner with André*. New York: Grove Press, 1981.

Shepard, Sam. *Fool for Love*. New York: Bantam Books, 1984.

————. *A Lie of the Mind*. New York: New American Library, 1986.

————. *Motel Chronicles*. San Francisco: City Lights Books, 1982.

Simon, Neil. *Brighton Beach Memoirs*. New York: Signet, 1984.

Stoppard, Tom. *The Real Thing*. London and Boston: Faber and Faber, 1984.

Therriault, Daniel. *Battery*. New York: Broadway Play Publishing, 1983.

Weller, Michael. *Ghost on Fire*. New York: Grove Press, 1987.

Wellman, John. *The Professional Frenchman*. In *Theatre of Wonders*. Los Angeles: Sun & Moon Press, 1985.

Willis, Jane. *Slam!* New York: Dramatists Play Service, 1985.

Wilson, August. *Fences*. New York: New American Library, 1986.

————. *Ma Rainey's Black Bottom*. New York: New American Library, 1985.

Wilson, Lanford. *Talley & Son*. New York: Hill & Wang, 1986.

Wolfe, George C. *The Colored Museum*. New York: Broadway Play Publishing, 1987.

Yankowitz, Susan. *A Knife in the Heart*. C/o The Author's Agent, Gloria Loomis, Watkins/Loomis Agency, 150 East 35 Street, New York, NY 10018.

* * * * *

Many of the above published titles are available by mail in major theatrical bookshops across the country. All titles are available and may be ordered through APPLAUSE THEATRE BOOKS, 211 West 71 Street, New York, NY 10023. Send $4 for a complete catalog. Or call (212) 595-4735.

ONE ON ONE

BEST MONOLOGUES FOR THE 90'S
Edited by Jack Temchin

You have finally met your match in Jack Temchin's new collection, *One on One*. Somewhere among the 150 monologues Temchin has recruited, a voice may beckon to you—strange and alluring—waiting for your own voice to give it presence on stage.

"The sad truth about most monologue books," says Temchin, "is that they don't give actors enough credit. I've compiled my book for serious actors with a passionate appetite for the unknown."

Among the selections:
David Mamer OLEANNA
Richard Greenberg THE AMERICAN PLAN
Brian Friel DANCING AT LUGHNASA
John Patrick Shanley THE BIG FUNK
Terrence McNally LIPS TOGETHER, TEETH APART
Neil Simon LOST IN YONKERS
David Hirson LA BETE
Herb Gardner CONVERSATIONS
WITH MY FATHER
Ariel Dorfman DEATH AND THE MAIDEN
Alan Ayckborn A SMALL FAMILY BUSINESS

$7.95 • paper
MEN: ISBN: 1-55783-151-3 • WOMEN: ISBN: 1-55783152-1

❧APPLAUSE❧